REVIVAL FOR MISSION

Mark A. Finley

Pacific Press®
Publishing Association

Nampa, Idaho | Oshawa, Ontario, Canada
www.pacificpress.com

Cover design by Gerald Lee Monks
Cover design resources from Lars Justinen
Inside design by Kristin Hansen-Mellish

The author assumes full responsibility for the accuracy of all facts and quotations as cited in this book.

Unless otherwise indicated, scriptures quoted in this book are from the New King James Version, copyright © 1979, 1980, 1982, Thomas Nelson, Inc., Publishers.

Scriptures quoted from AMP are from The Amplified Bible. Old Testament, copyright © 1965, 1987 by the Zondervan Corporation. The Amplified New Testament, copyright 1958, 1987 by the Lockman Foundation. Used by permission.

Scripture quotations marked KJV are from the King James Version.

Scripture quotations marked NIV are from the HOLY BIBLE, NEW INTERNA-TIONAL VERSION®. Copyright © 1973, 1978, 1984 by International Bible Society. Used by permission of Zondervan Publishing House. All rights reserved.

Scriptures quoted from Phillips are from J. B. Phillips: The New Testament in Modern English, Revised Edition, copyright © J. B. Phillips 1958, 1960, 1972. Used by permission of Macmillan Publishing Co., Inc.

You can obtain additional copies of this book by calling toll-free 1-800-765-6955 or by visiting http://www.adventistbookcenter.com.

Library of Congress Cataloging-in-Publication Data:

Finley, Mark, 1945–
  Revival for mission / Mark A. Finley.
     pages cm
  ISBN 13: 978-0-8163-4457-4 (pbk.)
  ISBN 10: 0-8163-4457-4 (pbk.)
  1. Religious awakening—Christianity. 2. Evangelistic work. 3. Missions.
4. Revivals. 5. Church renewal. I. Title.
  BV3790.F47 2013
  269—dc23   2013002343

13 14 15 16 17 • 5 4 3 2 1

Dedication

As I consider the men and women of God who have powerfully influenced my life and ministry over the past forty-five years, I realize that I have been greatly blessed. My mentors have shaped my thinking and set my spiritual direction.

Early in my ministry, Pastors John Tyndall, W. D. Frazee, and O. J. Mills were an incalculable influence. Later in my life, George Vandeman, Mikhail Kulakov, and Bob Spangler inspired me greatly. I will be eternally grateful for their influence.

This book is dedicated to these selfless preachers of revival who are now sleeping in Jesus—awaiting the outpouring of the Holy Spirit, the latter rain, the completion of God's mission, and the coming of Jesus.

Contents

Introduction

In every generation, God's Spirit works to bring revival to the hearts of His people. We can identify with the thoughts of the old hymn, "Come, Thou Fount of Every Blessing." The lines "Prone to wander, Lord, I feel it. / Prone to leave the God I love" echo in our minds. They drive us to our knees. Deep within the fabric of our being, we know they are true.

Our hearts *are* prone to wander. Our minds drift from the eternal to the mundane. Our thoughts turn so easily from the heavenly to the earthly. Too often we seem to be in bondage to deeply entrenched habits. At times our own attitudes and reactions baffle us. We want to do what's right, but we seem powerless to carry out our good intentions.

As the result of sin, our natures are fallen (Jeremiah 17:9). Our natural tendency is to turn from God's way to our own (Isaiah 53:6). With the apostle Paul, we, too, cry out, "O wretched man that I am!" (Romans 7:24). And with David, we plead, "Revive me, O Lord, according to your lovingkindness" (Psalm 119:159).

Revival is all about a God of loving-kindness seeking to deepen His relationship with us. Ellen White tells us:

> A revival and a reformation must take place, under the ministration of the Holy Spirit. Revival and reformation are two different things. Revival signifies a renewal of spiritual life, a quickening

of the powers of mind and heart, a resurrection from spiritual death. Reformation signifies reorganization, a change in ideas and theories, habits and practices. Reformation will not bring forth the good fruit of righteousness unless it is connected with the revival of the Spirit. Revival and reformation are to do their appointed work, and in doing this work they must blend.[1]

The initiative in revival is God's. His Spirit touches our hearts daily, creating spiritual longings within us. He convicts us of our need. He reveals God's life-changing goodness and grace. He empowers and sustains us, comforts and guides us, transforms and revives us. He reveals all we can be and all that through God's grace we will be.

Throughout history, God's Spirit has moved mightily in revival. At the dedication of the temple in Jerusalem, God spoke these words through Solomon, " 'If My people who are called by My name will humble themselves, and pray and seek My face, and turn from their wicked ways, then I will hear from heaven, and will forgive their sin and heal their land' " (2 Chronicles 7:14). And it was true. Centuries later, when Judah drifted from God's plan and purposes, God used the young king Josiah to lead the nation back to Himself, and a mighty revival followed. God's heart-longing was for His people to meet the conditions of revival and to experience the power it has to reveal the light of God's love to the entire world.

When God's people respond to His appeals, He works mightily in their behalf. This was true for the New Testament Christian church, at the time of the Reformation, and in the Advent movement. It will also be true for God's end-time people. His Holy Spirit will be poured out in its fullness, and the earth will be "illuminated with his glory" (Revelation 18:1).

Each chapter in this book focuses on the very essence of revival, reformation, and mission. Together we will discover answers to such questions as, What conditions has God given for the outpouring of His Spirit? Is God waiting for the arrival of some magical moment before He will pour out His Spirit on His last-day church? How can a person live a Spirit-filled life? What are the signs of a genuine revival, and how can we tell the difference between a genuine revival and a false revival?

And where does all revival and reformation ultimately lead?

Regarding the importance of revival, Ellen White said, "A revival of true godliness among us is the greatest and most urgent of all of our needs. To seek this should be our first work."[2] Heaven regards revival as having the highest priority. There is nothing more important.

The prophet Jeremiah attempted to shake those being held captive in Babylon out of the spiritual complacency they had settled into. He thundered the words of our Lord to the all-too-comfortable people: "You will seek Me and find Me, when you search for Me with all your heart" (Jeremiah 29:13). And later, Jesus also spoke of His people's urgent need of a revival that would lift them out of their cold, formal worship of God. He declared, " 'Seek first the kingdom of God and His righteousness, and all these things shall be added to you' " (Matthew 6:33).

There is nothing more urgent, nothing more important, nothing more significant than each of us being spiritually renewed daily. No congregation will experience corporate revival until its members have experienced personal, individual revival. God doesn't revive organizations. He revives people. "When churches are revived, it is because some individual seeks earnestly for the blessing of God. He hungers and thirsts after God, and asks in faith, and receives accordingly. He goes to work in earnest, feeling his great dependence upon the Lord, and souls are aroused to seek for a like blessing, and a season of refreshing falls on the hearts of men."[3]

As we explore prayer and revival, the Word and revival, witness and revival, a finished work and revival, and other related topics, God wants to speak powerfully to your heart. He wants to draw you closer to Him. Why not open your heart to the moving of His Spirit right now? Why not ask Him to do something extra special in your life? Why not ask Him to refresh your spiritual life so you can be an agent of revival in your home, your church, and your community? He will answer your prayers, and heaven's blessings will flow into your life in ways that you have never yet imagined.

1. Ellen G. White, *Review and Herald,* February 25, 1902.

2. White, *Selected Messages,* bk. 1 (Washington, D.C.: Review and Herald® Publishing Association, 1958), 121.

3. White, *Christian Service* (Washington, D.C.: Review and Herald®, 1947), 121.

CHAPTER 1

Revival: Our Great Need

What is a genuine spiritual revival? It is the reawakening of the dormant spiritual faculties of the soul. It occurs when we are passionate about knowing God. It happens when we are spiritually in tune with Him—when we listen to His commands and commit ourselves to obey them. It takes place when we allow God's Spirit to clear out all the clutter and distractions so we can truly hear God speak.

Ellen White describes revival this way:

> All who are under the training of God need the quiet hour for communion with their own hearts, with nature, and with God. In them is to be revealed a life that is not in harmony with the world, its customs, or its practices; and they need to have a personal experience in obtaining a knowledge of the will of God. We must individually hear Him speaking to the heart. When every other voice is hushed, and in quietness we wait before Him, the silence of the soul makes more distinct the voice of God. He bids us, "Be still, and know that I am God." Psalm 46:10. This is the effectual preparation for all labor for God. Amidst the hurrying throng, and the strain of life's intense activities, he who is thus refreshed will be surrounded with an atmosphere of light and peace. He will receive a new

endowment of both physical and mental strength. His life will breathe out a fragrance, and will reveal a divine power that will reach men's hearts.[1]

Revival demands a change in our priorities. It requires us to listen in humility to the voice of the Savior so that we know Him intimately and follow wherever He leads.

Laodicea's greatest need

Laodicea is the last in Revelation's sequence of seven churches. The name means "a people judged." Laodicea is a fitting symbol of God's last-day people. It was situated in an open valley in southwestern Turkey, beside one of the great trade routes to the east. This city was one of the great commercial and strategic centers of Asia Minor. It was a wealthy center of banking, of fashion, of education, and of medicine. Its inhabitants were independent, self-confident, rich—and extremely proud of their financial independence. When, in A.D. 61, an earthquake destroyed their city, they refused financial help from Rome, preferring to rebuild the city themselves.

The city's fashion industry was known throughout the area for the beautiful black woolen garments it produced, which were the envy of women throughout the Middle East. Its medical school developed a famous eye salve that was a popular cure for eye diseases.

The one vital natural resource that the city didn't have was water. The Laodiceans' water was piped via a Roman aqueduct from the hot springs in Hierapolis six miles away. By the time the water reached Laodicea, it was lukewarm.

Jesus used Laodicea as a symbol of His last-day church. His analysis should give us pause for reflection. Laodicea—Jesus' church in the end time—is described as self-confident, complacent, apathetic, and spiritually indifferent. It is a church that has lost its passion for lost people; a church whose members need a spiritual revival.

Nevertheless, Christ's message to Laodicea is filled with hope. He speaks to His people in tones of tender love, offering to meet their heart needs and to renew their deepest spiritual longings.

Hope for lukewarm Laodiceans

The titles Jesus used of Himself in His message to the church of Laodicea clearly communicate His willingness and ability to renew the spiritual life of lukewarm believers. Let's take a look at them.

"To the angel of the church of the Laodiceans write, 'These things says the Amen, the Faithful and True Witness, the Beginning of the creation of God' " (Revelation 3:14). In this verse, Jesus claims three titles. First, He says He is the "Amen." People use this word to express their agreement with what someone else has said and thus to "establish" the statement; to testify to its truthfulness. The apostle Paul echoes this thought in his epistle to the Corinthians. "All the promises of God in Him are Yes, and in Him Amen, to the glory of God through us" (2 Corinthians 1:20). Jesus confirms the truthfulness, the trustworthiness, of the gospel promises of forgiveness, divine power, salvation, and the infilling of the Holy Spirit. He is the Amen.

Second, Jesus is the "Faithful and True Witness" as to what the Father is like. He affirms His Father's love and grace. He reflects the Father's mind and character to fallen humanity. The greatest desire of both the Father and the Son is that the Laodiceans break out of their spiritual apathy and become Their friends. This is why Jesus said to His disciples, " 'No longer do I call you servants, for a servant does not know what his master is doing; but I have called you friends, for all things that I heard from My Father I have made known to you' " (John 15:15). This is good news for Laodicea. Though we Laodiceans are apathetic and spiritually indifferent, Jesus doesn't want to cast us off. Instead, He wants to charm us with His love, win us through His grace, and become our closest Friend. As the Faithful and True Witness, He reveals God's loving character.

Third, Jesus is also the "Beginning of the creation of God." In the Greek language in which John wrote, the word translated "beginning" is *archē*. It refers either to the point of time when something began or to the person who initiated something or some action. In this context, "beginning" refers to Jesus as the One who initiated and carried out all creation. He is the all-powerful Creator (John 1:1–3; Ephesians 3:8, 9). This is extremely significant. Jesus, the One who brought worlds and living beings

13

into existence merely by speaking, now speaks hope to Laodicea. The all-powerful Creator can create new life. He can create new spiritual longings in our hearts and transform our lives. That's why Paul wrote of Him, "If anyone is in Christ, he is a new creation; old things have passed away; behold, all things have become new" (2 Corinthians 5:17).

A loving rebuke

Next, Jesus tells the Laodiceans, " ' "I know your works, that you are neither cold nor hot. I could wish you were cold or hot. So then, because you are lukewarm, and neither cold nor hot, I will vomit you out of my mouth" ' " (Revelation 3:15, 16). The message to the church in Laodicea isn't an easy message to bear, especially if you take it personally. It's much easier to label others as being in a Laodicean condition than to think that we are too. As you reflect on the following passage, ask the Holy Spirit to help you apply it personally.

Ellen White commented: "The message to the Laodicean church applies most decidedly to those whose religious experience is insipid, who do not bear decided witness in favor of the truth."[2] An insipid religious experience is one that is lifeless. It has the external form of Christianity, but it lacks the substance, the living power. The Laodiceans weren't heretics or fiery fanatics. They were good moral people, but they were indifferent to spiritual things. Paul said they had "a form of godliness," but they denied its power (2 Timothy 3:5). Jesus spoke of a similar condition among the religious people He faced. He said, they " ' "draw near to Me with their mouth, and honor Me with their lips, but their heart is far from Me" ' " (Matthew 15:8). They have the outer husk of religion, but they've lost the kernel of faith.

But our Lord loves people too much to let them go easily. He'll do whatever it takes to kindle a spiritual flame in their hearts. His rebuke is strong only because His love is even stronger. He chastises only because He longs for us to heal. " 'Whom the LORD loves He chastens, and scourges every son whom He receives' " (Hebrews 12:6). The prophet Hosea echoes this sentiment in his call to repentance: "Come, and let us return to the LORD; for He has torn, but He will heal us; He has stricken, but He will bind us up" (Hosea 6:1).

Have you had times of trial that have drawn you closer to God? Has God ever humbled you with an embarrassing experience that has helped you recognize your need to depend on Him more? The Lord often allows us to go through these humbling experiences to help us see the difference between what we are and what He wants us to be. His rebukes in the form of life's trials and difficulties are revelations of our need of Him. When the comforts of an easy life muffle the voice of our Savior, preventing us from enjoying intimate fellowship with Him, the Holy Spirit longs to disturb our ease so we'll feel our need of Him and turn to Him again.

Perception and reality

There is a gap between the spiritual experience Laodicea thinks she has and the experience she actually has. Did you notice the precise wording of our Lord's indictment of Laodicea in Revelation 3:17? " 'You say, "I am rich, have become wealthy, and have need of nothing"—and do not know that you are wretched, miserable, poor, blind, and naked.' " Laodicea's problem isn't just that she doesn't know. It's that she doesn't know that she doesn't know. Laodicea's assessment of her own condition differs dramatically from God's assessment of it. One of Satan's most effective strategies in his attack upon us is to blind us to our spiritual condition.

But there is hope for Laodicea, and there is hope for all who are afflicted with spiritual apathy and indifference. Our Lord has the divine remedy for Laodicea's complacency. He offers us gold for our poverty, white raiment to cover our nakedness, and eye salve for our blindness. He advises us, " 'Buy from Me gold refined in the fire, that you may be rich; and white garments, that you may be clothed, that the shame of your nakedness may not be revealed; and anoint your eyes with eye salve, that you may see' " (verse 18). He invites us into a genuine experience with Him, one of ever-deepening trust. A superficial faith won't do. Make-believe religion and artificial spirituality are no match for the challenges of our times. Faith isn't developed in a crisis; it is revealed in a crisis. We have to develop it before the crisis breaks upon us.

In Revelation 3:18, Christ also tells us to buy from Him " 'white garments, that you may be clothed, that the shame of your nakedness may not be revealed.' " The "white garments" represent the "righteousness of the saints" (Revelation 19:8, KJV). Ellen White notes: "The white raiment is the righteousness of Christ that may be wrought into the character. Purity of heart, purity of motive, will characterize everyone who is washing his robe, and making it white in the blood of the Lamb."[3]

In Christ, we are forgiven. In Christ, we are cleansed. In Christ, we are new creatures. When we accept Him, we are in the center of His grace, and then, by faith, His righteousness becomes ours. Consequently, when the Father looks at us, He sees the perfect righteousness of His Son. As the old hymn says so well, "Rock of Ages, cleft for me, / Let me hide myself in Thee; / Let the water and the blood, . . . / Be of sin the double cure, / Cleanse me from its guilt and power." The righteousness of Jesus, which He offers so freely to His last-day church, delivers us from both the guilt and the power of sin.

Lastly, Jesus offers to anoint His people with eye salve so they can see. In the time of the Old Testament, the sanctuary and its furniture and priests were set apart, dedicated to serving God, in a divine service in which they were anointed. Jesus was set apart at His baptism, when the Holy Spirit anointed Him. Laodicea needs divine discernment so she can see that she has been set apart, or totally consecrated, to her Master for the purpose of bringing glory to His name. When the Holy Spirit anoints our eyes, we are able to see defects in our characters that we have never seen before. We are able to see ourselves in a new light. With Job we cry out, " 'I abhor myself, and repent in dust and ashes' " (Job 42:6). With Isaiah, we cry, " 'Woe is me, for I am undone!' " (Isaiah 6:5). And with Daniel, we pray, "We have sinned and committed iniquity, we have done wickedly and rebelled, even by departing from Your precepts and Your judgments" (Daniel 9:5).

This new vision of ourselves opens our eyes to a new vision of Christ as well. Unless we see ourselves as we are, we will never see Him as He really is. When we see our sinfulness, we long for His holiness. When we understand our unrighteousness, we seek His righteousness. This new vision of ourselves doesn't depress us; it motivates us to seek Christ with all of our hearts, for we know He alone can satisfy our deepest needs. When the scales fall from our eyes, we see Him standing before us, longing to have a deeper relationship with us than we thought possible.

> Jesus is going from door to door, standing in front of every soul-temple, proclaiming, "I stand at the door, and knock." As a heavenly merchantman, he opens his treasures, and cries, "Buy of me gold tried in the fire, that thou mayest be rich; and white raiment, that thou mayest be clothed, and that the shame of thy nakedness do not appear." The gold he offers is without alloy, more precious than that of Ophir; for it is faith and love. The white raiment he invites the soul to wear is his own robes of righteousness, and the oil for anointing is the oil of his grace, which will give spiritual eyesight to the soul in blindness and darkness, that he may distinguish between the workings of the Spirit of God and the spirit of the enemy. Open your doors, says the great Merchantman, the possessor of spiritual riches, and transact your business with me. It is I, your Redeemer, who counsels you to buy of me.[4]

A relentless love

The message to the church in Laodicea ends with an earnest, heart-felt appeal. Jesus says to each of us, " ' " 'Behold, I stand at the door and knock. If anyone hears My voice and opens the door, I will come in to him and dine with him, and he with Me. To him who overcomes I will grant to sit with Me on My throne, as I also overcame and sat down with My Father on His throne' " ' " (Revelation 3:20, 21).

In the Middle East, the evening meal was (and still is) extremely important. When the work of the day was over and the men returned from the fields, the entire family gathered around the table. In most instances, the extended family lived in close proximity, so at times the number of people at the evening meal often would be quite large. Grandfather and grandmother, brothers and sisters, aunts and uncles, nephews and nieces and cousins all gathered together. In this grand reunion after a hard day's work and on special occasions, stories were told, experiences were shared, and counsel was given. It was a time of fellowship. It was a time of warmth and family intimacy.

Jesus longs to have this kind of fellowship with you. There is a place in His heart that no one but you can fill (see Psalms 33:15; 139:17, 18; Isaiah 43:1–3). Jesus longs to be your Friend. He wants you to share the secrets of your heart with Him. You can feel secure in His presence. The One who knows all about you loves you more than you can ever imagine.

More than anything else, Jesus wants to spend eternity with us. The book of Revelation mentions God's throne thirty-seven times. That's more than any other book of the Bible mentions it. God's throne is mentioned in fourteen of Revelation's twenty-two chapters. We read of "a rainbow around the throne," "lightnings" proceeding from the throne, "lamps of fire . . . before the throne," "angels around the throne," "God who sits on the throne," and "the Lamb who is in the midst of the throne" (Revelation 4:3, 5; 5:11; 7:10, 17). At God's throne, we join in with the inhabitants of heaven and joyously proclaim, " 'Worthy is the Lamb who was slain to receive power and riches and wisdom, and strength and honor and glory and blessing!' " (Revelation 5:12). God promises that we can participate in heaven's rejoicing when the long saga of sin comes to a close.

Christ makes His most powerful appeal to Laodicea, His end-time church. His love has moved Him to provide eternity for us. We have royal blood running through our veins. We are sons and daughters of the King of the universe. We can reign with Him, sit with Him upon His throne forever and ever.

It is this love that makes God long to spend all eternity with us. This love constitutes the greatest motivation for us to wake from our spiritual slumber. If this isn't enough to shake us out of our spiritual apathy, what is? If this isn't enough to send us to our knees seeking revival, nothing else is either.

---

1. Ellen G. White, *The Ministry of Healing* (Mountain View, Calif.: Pacific Press® Publishing Association, 1942), 58.

2. White, in *The Seventh-day Adventist Bible Commentary,* ed. Francis D. Nichol (Washington, D.C.: Review and Herald®, 1980), 7:962.

3. White, *Review and Herald,* July 24, 1888.

4. Ibid., August 7, 1894.

CHAPTER 2

Prayer: The Heartbeat of Revival

Teenagers have a way of surprising you with their penetrating questions. John's questions certainly surprised me. "Pastor, how long do you pray? I mean, how many hours each day do you spend with God?"

I wondered whether John would judge my spirituality by the amount of time I spent praying. But my young friend was really asking a much deeper question than that of time. He was asking, "How can I know God? How can I experience His presence and power in my life? How can I have a meaningful relationship with Him?"

The Bible presents a God who longs to know us more than we long to know Him. His heart yearns for a relationship with His lost children. When we kneel in prayer, we are kneeling before the all-knowing God of the universe—but we are also kneeling before One who longs to enjoy the fellowship of our presence.

Ellen White put it this way: "Prayer is the opening of the heart to God as to a friend. Not that it is necessary in order to make known to God what we are, but in order to enable us to receive Him. Prayer does not bring God down to us, but brings us up to Him."[1] This statement contains two especially significant insights about prayer. First, it isn't a matter of keeping track of how much time we're praying. It's about a relationship with a friend, and friends spend time together because they enjoy being with each other. Having said that, however, we must admit that consistency in our prayer life is critically important. It is difficult to maintain a close relationship with someone with whom you rarely spend any time. Jesus bathed His life in prayer (see, e.g., Mark 1:35; Luke 5:16). He spent time with His Father.

How much do I pray? I don't evaluate my prayer life by how many minutes or hours I spend praying. I evaluate it, measure it, by how it affects my relationship with God. I aim to enter the presence of God every day. The time I spend in my devotions varies. The critical question isn't "How long have I spent praying today?" It is "Have I had fellowship with God today?" Revival is all about knowing God. It is all about having a meaningful relationship with Him through prayer, Bible study, and witness. Without earnest, heartfelt prayer, there can be no revival.

Alfred, Lord Tennyson was certainly right when he said, "More things are wrought by prayer than this world dreams of." The great revivals Scripture tells us about were conceived through prayer. The Old Testament records prayers in which Moses, David, and Daniel petitioned the Almighty for power from on high. Jesus' prayer life reveals His constant dependence on His heavenly Father. The Gospels indicate that it was when He was on His knees and alone with the Father that He received the most strength. And even a casual reading of the book of Acts reveals New Testament believers storming heaven on their knees, seeking the outpouring of the Holy Spirit.

Closer to our time, Ellen White wrote about the earnest intercession that took place as she met with the other Adventist pioneers to seek truth. "At our important meetings," she wrote, "these men would meet together and search for the truth as for hidden treasure. I met with them, and we studied and prayed earnestly; for we felt that we must learn God's truth. Often we remained together until late at night, and sometimes through the entire night, praying for light, and studying the Word. As we fasted and prayed, great power came upon us."[2] These faithful men and women of God recognized that they could know Christ and His truth and live the principles of His kingdom only as they were absolutely dependent upon God.

An acknowledgment of our need

Prayer is an acknowledgment of our need. It is through prayer that we open our hearts to receive the blessings of heaven. It isn't some reluctance on God's part that restrains the outpouring of His Holy Spirit upon us. What hinders its release is our lack of readiness to receive the heavenly gift. In our times of prayer, the Holy Spirit convicts us of attitudes and actions that hinder His mighty outpouring through us. When we pray, our hearts are open to all God wants to do for us.

The twentieth-century revivalist Leonard Ravenhill put it this way: "True revival changes the moral climate of an area or a nation. . . . Without exception, all true revivals of the past began after years of agonizing, hell-robbing, earth-shaking, heaven-sent intercession."[3]

R. A. Torrey was a powerful preacher of revival in the late nineteenth and early twentieth centuries. He conducted revival meetings in Great Britain between 1903 and 1905 and throughout North America in 1906 and 1907. Lamenting the busyness of Christians, he stated, "We are too busy to pray, and so we are too busy to have power. We have a great deal of activity, but we accomplish little; many services but few conversions; much machinery but few results."[4]

It was prayer that underlay the exploits of faith recorded in the book of Acts. The disciples met together for ten days, during which they earnestly sought the promise of the Holy Spirit (Acts 1:14). And then three thousand converts joined them and "continued steadfastly in the apostles' doctrine and fellowship, in the breaking of bread, and in prayers" (Acts 2:41, 42).

The early church chose deacons so the apostles could give themselves " 'continually to prayer and to the ministry of the Word' " (Acts 6:4). When Peter prayed, God opened a way for the early church to reach the Gentiles. And when the entire church interceded, he was miraculously released from prison (see Acts 10 and 12).

The disciples' experience with prayer in the upper room launched them into a life of prayer that continued throughout the believers' entire ministry as recorded in the book of Acts. Through prayer, they developed trusting hearts. Through prayer, they learned to depend on the Almighty. Through prayer, they acknowledged their weakness and sought His strength. Through prayer, they admitted their ignorance and sought His wisdom. Through prayer, the disciples recognized their limitations and cried out for God's all-sufficient power. Pentecost was the result of heartfelt intercession.

Acts pictures believers as being filled with power from on high. The Holy Spirit was poured out in a marked way. Hearts were touched. Lives were changed. The gospel penetrated the most difficult places, and tens of thousands were converted. Acts 2 says that three thousand were added to the church (verse 41); Acts 4:4 records that five thousand men believed; and if we add women and children, the number certainly must have been between fifteen and twenty thousand. Even many of the religious leaders who had not openly accepted Jesus during His lifetime became "obedient to the faith" (Acts 6:7).

The story of this phenomenal growth continues in Acts 9, where we read that churches throughout "all Judea, Galilee, and Samaria" were "multiplied" (verse 31). And then, as Jesus had said would be the case, the gospel flame lit in the Jerusalem leapt across even larger cultural and geographical boundaries. Acts 8 tells the story of the baptism of the treasurer of Ethiopia, and in a more extensive report, Acts 10 and 11 note the conversion of the Roman centurion Cornelius and his family and the impact that had on the infant church.

So, Acts tells us the story of the growth of the church. The first chapter records that after Jesus' ascension, some thirty years into the first century A.D., 120 believers met in the upper room (verse 15). The best estimates are that by the end of that century, some seventy years later, there were at least one million Christians in the Roman Empire. This is remarkable growth by any standard.

With open hearts

Through prayer, we open our hearts to everything Jesus has for us. We lay our souls bare to receive the fullness of His power. One of the prime characteristics of healthy relationships is communication—people who care about each other want to talk to each other. That's true of our relationship with God too: if we care about Him and believe He cares about us, we want to communicate with Him just as we would with any other close friend or companion. The upper room was a place of communion with God—a place where the disciples prayed individually and together in corporate prayer. They "met together to present their requests to the Father in the name of Jesus. They knew that they had a Representative in heaven, an Advocate at the throne of God. In solemn awe they bowed in prayer, repeating the assurance, 'Whatsoever ye shall ask the Father in My name, He will give it you. Hitherto have ye asked nothing in My name; ask, and ye shall receive, that your joy may be full.' John 16:23, 24."[5]

We have the same Representative in heaven as did the first disciples. He invites us, as He did them, to bring our burdens to Him. We have the same Friend positioned at the throne of God. He urges us as He did those who served Him two thousand years ago to present the longings of our hearts to Him. We, too, can claim His promises. We, too, can extend our hand of faith higher and higher. We, too, can ask Him to bestow heaven's most priceless gift, the Holy Spirit, upon us.

We are living at a special time in human history. All heaven invites us to grasp the promises of the Almighty. God longs to do something special for His church now. He invites us to seek Him with all our hearts so we receive the power of His Holy Spirit in the latter rain that will enable us to finish the work He has commissioned us to do. Our Lord's promises are as true today as they were two thousand years ago. If we meet the conditions, He will answer from heaven. He has pledged Himself to give us what we must have to carry out that task. When we kneel before Him each morning, we can claim His promise that He will give us the refreshing, renewing power of His Spirit.

Here is another encouraging promise that we can claim by faith as we pray: "Morning by morning, as the heralds of the gospel kneel before the Lord and renew their vows of consecration to Him, He will grant them the presence of His Spirit, with its reviving, sanctifying power. As they go forth to the day's duties, they have the assurance that the unseen agency of the Holy Spirit enables them to be 'laborers together with God.' "[6]

Prayer makes a difference. Through prayer we enter into fellowship with Jesus and are filled with His Holy Spirit. Jesus' life, His example, reveals the necessity of our living lives of unbroken communion with God. We learn from His prayer life what it means to really know God.

Jesus' prayer life

Jesus is our great Model in intercession. He regularly retreated to quiet places where He could pray. He prayed for strength to meet the challenges of the day. He pleaded with His Father for strength to overcome Satan's temptations. The Gospel of Mark mentions one of Jesus' early morning prayer sessions: "In the morning, having risen a long while before daylight, He went out and departed to a solitary place; and there He prayed" (Mark 1:35). If Jesus, the Divine Son of God, thought He needed to pray, how much more do we need what prayer supplies?

Our Lord recognized that spiritual strength comes through prayer. Luke wrote, "He Himself often withdrew into the wilderness and prayed" (Luke 5:16). Jesus didn't pray just occasionally—just when a need or problem arose. Prayer was a vital part of His life. It was the key to staying connected to the Father. It was the essence of vibrant spirituality. Jesus' prayer life gave Him courage and strength to face temptation. He came from these prayer sessions refreshed spiritually and with a renewed commitment to do the Father's will.

Describing one of these prayer times, Luke notes that as Jesus "prayed, the appearance of His face was altered, and His robe became white and glistening" (Luke 9:29), Jesus radiated the strength that comes from moments spent in God's presence through prayer. If Jesus, the Divine Son of God, considered time in His Father's presence essential to His overcoming the fierce temptations of Satan, we can only imagine how much greater is our need!

Jesus never considered Himself too busy to pray. He never thought His schedule so full that He didn't have time to commune with His Father. He never felt He had so much to do that He must rush into and then out of His Father's presence.

Jesus came from the intimate times He spent with God spiritually revived. He was filled with power because He took time to pray.

Christ was continually receiving from the Father, that he might communicate to us. "The word which ye hear," he said, "is not mine, but the Father's which sent me." "The Son of man came not to be ministered unto, but to minister." Not for himself, but for others, he lived and thought and prayed. From hours spent with God he came forth morning by morning, to bring the light of heaven to men. Daily he received a fresh baptism of the Holy Spirit. In the early hours of the new day the Lord awakened him from his slumbers, and his soul and his lips were anointed with grace, that he might impart to others.[7]

The Gospel of Mark provides us with some other important insights into Jesus' prayer life. "Now in the morning, having risen a long while before daylight, He went out and departed to a solitary place; and there He prayed" (Mark 1:35). There are two specific things to note about this passage. Jesus had a *time* to pray, and He had a *place* to pray. He didn't leave His prayer life to chance.

Most of us have regular times to eat. Do we have as regular a time to spend with God? A time when you allow nothing to disturb you? And do you have a place where you can pray undisturbed? A place you can be alone with God?

Scripture also indicates that Jesus sometimes prayed aloud. Matthew says that when He was pleading with the Father to find a way to avoid Calvary, He "fell on His face, and prayed, *saying . . .*" (Matthew 26:39; emphasis added; cf. verses 42, 44). And Hebrews says that in Gethsemane, Jesus "offered up prayers and supplications, with *vehement cries* and tears to Him who was able to save Him from death" (Hebrews 5:7; emphasis added). Praying out loud focuses our thoughts and helps us keep our minds from wandering. This is why Ellen White counsels us to "learn to pray aloud where only God can hear you."[8]

Don't misunderstand me. There certainly are times when it is appropriate to pray silently. I often offer silent petitions to God. But if you long for closer fellowship with Jesus, find a quiet place and pour your heart out to Him aloud.

As you pray aloud, Jesus will draw near, and all the evil angels will flee.[9]

Praying together

Although at times Jesus prayed by Himself, there were multiple oc-casions when He encouraged His closest disciples to pray with Him. (See, e.g., Luke 9:18.) Peter, James, and John accompanied Jesus to the Mount of Transfiguration (Matthew 17:1, 2). And when Jesus was praying in Gethsemane, He urged them to pray with Him (Matthew 26:36, 37, 40, 41; Luke 22:39–46).

When people pray together, they receive extraordinary power. Jesus urged His disciples to pray together with their hearts in one accord. He admonished, " 'Again I say to you that if two of you agree on earth concerning anything that they ask, it will be done for them by My Father in heaven. For where two or three are gathered in My name, I am there in the midst of them' " (Matthew 18:19, 20).

The original Greek word translated "agree" here means "in com-plete accord." This word was used of varied voices blended together in a symphony of song. When we are united in prayer, with hearts in one accord, our voices become a chorus of praise testifying to the power of the gospel. This joyful melody brings gladness to Jesus' heart. When we're united in prayer, one member's strong faith can compensate for another's shortsightedness, one's strength helps another's weakness, one's meekness counterbalances another's forwardness, and one's might aids another's frailty. When united in prayer, members share common joys and sorrows, strengths and weaknesses, joys and heartaches.

Christ promises two specific things for those who are united in prayer. First, He promises that when we approach Him in united prayer with hearts desiring only His glory, He will answer. When we come jointly in prayer, seeking His will, longing to know Him better, and asking for the outpouring of His Spirit on us and those for whom we're praying, He will answer powerfully. Miracles beyond our comprehen-sion will be wrought.

Second, Christ promises that when we approach Him with united hearts and in His name, He'll be in our midst. This implies not only that the people who are praying are united with one another, but also that they are united with Christ. These praying believers are seeking more of His love; they're yearning to feel His presence; and they're desiring that He be glorified in what they're requesting. Christ's praying disciples have the joy of knowing that He is really present with them.

God respects our freedom of choice. Although He works graciously in our lives even before we approach Him in prayer, when we do pray, we give our all-powerful Creator, loving Redeemer, and coming King, Jesus Christ, permission to use us to glorify His name in any way He desires.

---

1. Ellen G. White, *Steps to Christ* (Washington, D.C.: Review and Herald®, 1956), 93.

2. White, *Manuscript Releases* (Silver Spring, Md.: Ellen G. White Estate, 1990), 3:207.

3. Leonard Ravenhill, *Revival God's Way* (Bloomington, Minn.: Bethany House Publishers, 1986), quoted in Day 6 of "2013 Heart-Cry for Revival Conference Prayer Guide," Heart-Cry for Revival, accessed March 27, 2013, http://heart-cryforrevival.org/content/2013prayday6.

4. R. A. Torrey, quoted in "Prayer and Intercession Quote," Tentmaker Ministries, accessed March 27, 2013, http://www.tentmaker.org/Quotes/prayerquotes5.htm.

5. White, *The Acts of the Apostles* (Mountain View, Calif.: Pacific Press®, 1911), 36.

6. Ibid., 56.

7. White, *Review and Herald,* August 11, 1910.

8. White, *Our High Calling* (Washington, D.C.: Review and Herald®, 1961), 130.

9. See White, *Counsels for the Church* (Nampa, Idaho: Pacific Press®, 1991), 319.

The Word: The Foundation of Revival

Recently, the General Conference of Seventh-day Adventists launched an initiative titled Revived by His Word. The church members around the world who joined this movement studied one chapter of the Bible each day. The life-changing results of this initiative are remarkable. Here is just a sampling of the thousands of testimonies sent in to the General Conference:

"As I read God's Word I feel more connected with God. I have learned to listen to Him."—Valere

"Reading God's Word has changed my life. . . . I used to be violent and always aggressive, but . . . because of God's words and His love, I'm now peaceful, loving, and kind."—Will

"For the first time in my life I feel closer to God. . . . It is the best help that our church has ever given me. . . . Thank you!"—Joan

"God's Word . . . has brought a big change in my life. . . . It sharpens my mind and has a calming effect on me."—Abegail

"I'm definitely seeing a difference in my life. . . . It's a great feeling to get up in the morning knowing that I'm going to be revived by His Word."—Judith

These testimonies, along with tens of thousands of others, are evidence of the effectiveness of Ellen White's prescription: "A revival in Bible study is needed throughout the world. Attention is to be called, not to the assertions of men, but to the Word of God. As this is done, a mighty work will be wrought."[1]

Unless accompanied by a systematic study of God's Word, any emphasis on revival and reformation will die out quickly, degenerate into sentimental slogans, or result in a counterfeit spiritual experience. The study of God's Word that leads to a life-changing experience with Jesus is not optional in a revival; it is foundational. Nothing can possibly replace listening to God speak to us through His Word. Prayerfully meditating on Scripture is a primary source of spiritual strength.

Revival through the centuries

Throughout Psalms, David testifies to the blessings of the Word that he has experienced. He found courage and strength in God's Word, and he discovered hope and divine guidance there. The Word of God brought light to his darkened mind (Psalm 119:130). It nourished his famished heart and quenched his thirsty soul (verse 81). When Saul threatened to kill him, he clung to God's promise of deliverance (Psalm 34:4). Plagued with guilt after his adulterous affair with Bathsheba, he clung to God's promise of forgiveness (Psalm 32:1, 2). Perplexed regarding the future, he trusted in God's promise of guidance (verse 8). Eventually, he was able to exclaim jubilantly, "Your word has given me life" (Psalm 119:50)! Revival is all about finding new life in God's Word.

At Pentecost, the Holy Spirit was poured out upon a praying group of disciples who believed the Word of God implicitly. By faith they had grasped the Savior's promise, accepted His word, and waited for its fulfillment. Filled with confidence in their Savior, these New Testament believers went out and changed the world (see Acts 4:31; Colossians 1:23–26).

The Reformation was also a revival movement deeply rooted in Scripture. In the seclusion and tranquility of the Piedmont valleys of northern Italy and southern France during the thirteenth and fourteenth centuries after Christ, Waldensian parents filled the minds of their children with the teachings of the Word. Handwritten copies of the Bible were treasured, and large portions of it were memorized. Many of these young people were sent as missionaries to the great universities of Europe. As they opened the sacred truths of God's Word to others in those institutions, spiritual revivals broke out.

In later years, the Bible formed the basis for the preaching of Huss, Jerome, Luther, Zwingli, Calvin, Whitefield, and Wesley. The blazing light of Scripture exposed the manmade dogmas of the medieval church for what they were, and the Spirit-filled proclamation of the Word of God transformed the lives of tens of thousands of people who had been held captive by the shackles of superstition.

The nineteenth-century Advent movement was a revival movement bathed in God's Word. With the Bible as the foundation of their faith, those early Adventists proclaimed with urgency the need to prepare for the coming of Jesus, triggering a revival that changed the course of human history. The same Holy Spirit who inspired the Bible still transforms those who read it.

Revelation's prophecies indicate that the serious Bible study that spawned revival movements in the past will do so again (see Revelation 12:17; 14:6–12). God will once again raise up a generation of committed Christians who are passionate about discovering His will in His Word. They will find grace and strength and hope in His Word. They'll come face-to-face with the matchless charms of Christ in His Word. In the light of God's love, His people will experience a mighty spiritual revival. The Holy Spirit will be poured out beyond measure, and the gospel will be carried to the ends of the earth (Matthew 24:14; Revelation 18:1).

The Word's creative power

God's Word is creative. At Creation, His audible word became tangible matter—the syllables proceeding from His mouth formed the things they named. Thus the earth appeared at His command—as did the sun, moon, and stars, and all living things.

This same creative power is found in God's Written Word. As we'll see, Hebrews 4:12 is packed with meaning. Each phrase is significant. We'll examine each part and determine its meaning for our lives today.

"The word of God is living and powerful, and sharper than any two-edged sword." The Bible is the Written Word, and Jesus is the Living Word—the Word made flesh (see John 1:1, 14). So, if you want to see what the Written Word looks like applied in our world, look at Jesus.

Scripture also is a creative Word (see Psalm 33:6, 9). God's Word is powerful. The Greek word translated as "powerful" is *energēs,* from which we get the word *energy.* As Ellen White so aptly states it, "The creative energy that called the worlds into existence is in the word of God. This word imparts power; it begets life. Every command is a promise; accepted by the will, received into the soul, it brings with it the life of the Infinite One. It transforms the nature and re-creates the soul in the image of God."[2] As we study the Bible with a meditative mind and a prayerful attitude, the creative power that brought the world into existence will transform our lives.

The writer of Hebrews declares that the Word of God is "sharper than any two-edged sword, *piercing even to the division of soul and spirit, and of joints and marrow, and is a discerner of the thoughts and intents of the heart*" (Hebrews 4:12; emphasis added). Three interesting couplets follow in our text: "soul and spirit," "joints and marrow," and "thoughts and intents." "Soul and spirit" represent our spiritual faculties; "joints and marrow," our physical abilities, and "thoughts and intents," our mental capacities. In the hands of the Divine Surgeon, the Word of the Living God cuts away the cancers of our souls. It cuts through our selfishness and pride. It cuts through all the sham and pretense of religiosity, and it lays bare our souls' need of Jesus' transforming grace.

The point of this text is that the Word of God can transform our entire nature. It governs every aspect of human life and behavior— sinful attitudes, long-established habits, and both the cultivated and the inherited tendencies toward evil that extend deep within the fabric of our being. Grace is greater, more powerful, than sin. The creative power that flows through God's Word changes us forever.

There is value in listening to wise human counsel. We have all been helped at times by the advice of our friends. However, human advice doesn't have the power to change us. God's Word, on the other hand, is a living, dynamic, powerful change agent. The same power that was in the words God spoke at Creation is in His Written Word. When we by faith accept God's commands and promises, we receive the power of the Holy Spirit as well. So, the Bible doesn't just tell us how to live. As we open our minds and hearts to the Holy Spirit's guidance, the power of God's creative Word will flow into our lives, enabling us to actually believe His promises and live our lives accordingly.

Jesus and the Word

Pentecost changed the disciples dramatically. Before Pentecost, their young faith often faltered. After Pentecost, it was rock solid. The outpouring of the Holy Spirit strengthened the disciples to face the opposition that came as they proclaimed Jesus' love and grace. Before Pentecost, Peter cowered in fear in the high priest's courtyard when Jesus was brought there to be tried, and he denied Jesus with the cowardly lie, " 'I do not know the Man!' " (Matthew 26:72). At that time, Peter's faith was fragile and vacillating. But on the Day of Pentecost, Peter powerfully pointed out the Old Testament evidence that Jesus was the Messiah.

Compare also Peter's denial in the courtyard before Pentecost to his response to the Jewish authorities who tried to silence his voice after that fateful day. To them he boldly declared, " 'We cannot but speak the things which we have seen and heard' " (Acts 4:20). The indwelling of the fullness of the Holy Spirit made all the difference. In his own strength, Peter was no match for the cunning devices of the enemy. But with Jesus' strength, he was more than able to live for God.

The apostle Paul prayed that the Ephesians might have this empowerment of the Holy Spirit—he said he was praying that God "would grant you, according to the riches of His glory, to be strengthened with might through His Spirit in the inner man" (Ephesians 3:16).

Faith grasps the promise of the Holy Spirit as a divine reality. It believes Christ's promise that He will grant His Holy Spirit abundantly. In fact, "faith that enables us to receive God's gifts is itself a gift, of which some measure is imparted to every human being. It grows as exercised in appropriating the Word of God. In order to strengthen faith, we must often bring it in contact with the word."[3] As we behold Jesus through His Word, the Spirit who inspired the Word grows our faith (see Romans 10:17).

In reality, "faith is trusting God—believing that He loves us and knows best what is for our good. Thus, instead of our own, it leads us to choose His way. In place of our ignorance, it accepts His wisdom; in place of our weakness, His strength; in place of our sinfulness, His righteousness. Our lives, ourselves, are already His; faith acknowledges His ownership and accepts its blessing. Truth, uprightness, purity, have been pointed out as secrets of life's success. It is faith that puts us in possession of these principles."[4]

Faith is believing that God loves us and always has our best good in mind. Through faith the Holy Spirit leads us to grasp the magnitude of the gift of grace offered so freely on Calvary. Through faith we receive spiritual strength to resist the temptations of the evil one. Through faith we are empowered to witness. Through faith we are motivated to do whatever Jesus asks and to obey whatever He commands. Faith grasps the promises of God and believes that they are meant for us.

At Pentecost, the disciples "higher and still higher . . . extended the hand of faith" and "under the Holy Spirit's working even the weakest, by exercising faith in God, learned to improve their entrusted powers and to become sanctified, refined, and ennobled."[5] This experience can be ours too. The Holy Spirit longs to both deepen and increase our faith.

Here are three practical ways to increase your faith. First, expect the Holy Spirit to grow your faith as you study God's Word. Approach your Bible study with a sense of expectation. Believe that the Spirit who inspired the Bible is going to make miraculous changes in your life as you persist in studying the Word. (See 2 Peter 1:3, 4.)

Second, apply God's Word to your life. To receive the benefit of Bible study, we must apply it to our lives individually. Put yourself in the story. What lessons is the Holy Spirit revealing to you in the text of Scripture? What insights for daily living is He revealing? What convictions is He bringing to your mind?

Third, act on the "measure of faith" that God has already placed in your heart. Look beyond the current circumstances of your life to the blessings God has for you in the near future. If the Holy Spirit impresses you to do something, do it believing you will be richly rewarded as you act on His Word.

Our spiritual experience is revived when we accept and claim the promises in God's Word by faith. There is little benefit derived from hastily reading the Bible out of a sense of obligation or duty. We are changed as we internalize what we are reading and allow the teachings of the Bible to mold our thoughts and shape our lives.

The Word of God bears witness of Jesus. (See, e.g., John 5:39; 15:26; 16:14, 15.) The Holy Spirit also bears witness of Jesus. The Spirit leads us to a deeper experience with Jesus as we read His Word. The purpose of the Holy Spirit is not primarily to manifest Himself through doing supernatural signs and wonders; rather, it is to exalt Jesus through His Word. The point isn't the great miracles *we* can do. The point is *His* power to transform lives. Jesus declared, " 'It is the Spirit who gives life; the flesh profits nothing. The words that I speak to you are spirit, and they are life' " (John 6:63). The plain meaning of Jesus' statement is that the power of the Holy Spirit flows through His Word to bring us spiritual life.

True revival

What role does truth play in revival? What about our experience? How does revival relate to our feelings and our emotions?

The story of Jesus' appearance to the two disciples on the road to Emmaus reveals the role the Bible plays in producing true revival in the hearts of Christ's followers. Those two disciples of Christ were filled with confusion. They were perplexed about the future, and their hearts were troubled. When Jesus joined them on their journey, they didn't notice who He was. Then, gradually, He "expounded to them in all the Scriptures the things concerning Himself" (Luke 24:27).

Jesus could have worked a miracle to prove His identity, but He didn't. He could have shown them the scars in His hands as soon as He started walking with them, but He didn't. Instead, He gave them a Bible study on prophecy.

Notice what these two disciples said when they reflected on what had happened that day: "They said to one another, 'Did not our heart burn within us while He talked with us on the road, and while He opened the Scriptures to us?' " (Luke 24:32)

What an example of genuine revival! Jesus appealed to these disciples on the basis of Scripture. Their hearts burned within them, and they jogged back to Jerusalem to tell their story, praising God all the way. Their experience was anchored in the Word of God.

If we want revival in our day, we must stop giving excuses and fill our minds with the Word. One of heaven's conditions for revival is the commitment to live a life based on its principles.

Understanding the Bible better

Here are two Spirit-inspired principles that will transform your study of the Bible. First, approach the Bible with a sense of both reverence and excitement. The Bible is a gift from God, and the same Holy Spirit who inspired the Bible originally will inspire you as you read it. Come to God's Word with a sense of anticipation, believing that He will speak to you through His Holy Spirit as you read His Word. (See 2 Timothy 3:16; 2 Peter 1:21; John 6:63.)

Second, in the frantic pace of our twenty-first-century living, the prophet Isaiah reminds us, "Thus says the Lord GOD, the Holy One of Israel: 'In returning and rest you shall be saved; in quietness and confidence shall be your strength' " (Isaiah 30:15). It does seem that in these fast-paced days, genuine Christian meditation on God's Word is becoming a lost art. Thoughtfully opening God's Word, reading a few verses, meditating upon His love, contemplating His character, and reflecting upon His greatness is life changing. The Holy Spirit speaks to us in these quiet moments.

Why not take a few quiet moments today to open your Bible, to ask God to speak to you through His Word, to read a few verses, to meditate upon what God is saying to you, and to let Him speak to you. When you make prayerful Bible study a lifelong habit, it will change your life. Then the amazing promise below from God's last-day messenger to His end-time church will be fulfilled in your life. She wrote

35

that in all the promises of God's Word, "He is speaking to us individually, speaking as directly as if we could listen to His voice. It is in these promises that Christ communicates to us His grace and power. They are leaves from that tree which is 'for the healing of the nations.' Revelation 22:2. Received, assimilated, they are to be the strength of the character, the inspiration and sustenance of the life. Nothing else can have such healing power. Nothing besides can impart the courage and faith which give vital energy to the whole being."[6]

---

1. Ellen G. White, *Evangelism* (Washington, D.C.: Review and Herald®, 1946), 456.
2. White, *Education* (Mountain View, Calif.: Pacific Press®, 1952), 126.
3. Ibid., 254; see also Romans 12:3.
4. Ibid., 253.
5. White, *The Acts of the Apostles,* 36, 49, 50.
6. White, *The Ministry of Healing,* 122.

CHAPTER 4

Witness and Service:
The Passion of Revival

Revival must be an ongoing part of the spiritual journey of each Christian. That means we must renew our commitment to Jesus every day. Doing so leads us into a deepening experience in prayer, a more diligent study of God's Word, and a life of service and witness.

Shortly before His death, Jesus prayed, " 'This is eternal life, that they may know You, the only true God, and Jesus Christ whom You have sent' " (John 17:3). Revival is about knowing Jesus intimately. It is about fellowship with Him. Genuine revivals awaken our hearts to His goodness, His compassion, His forgiveness, and His power.

And when we are charmed by Jesus' love and transformed by His grace, we won't be able to stay silent. Jesus' love will overflow from our lives to the lives of others. As we share His love with them, we ourselves will be drawn nearer to Him, and the more we share His love, the more we will love Him. So, mission is not only the *goal* of revival; it is also the *means* of revival. "God could have reached His object in saving sinners without our aid; but in order for us to develop a character like Christ's, we must share in His work. In order to enter into His joy,— the joy of seeing souls redeemed by His sacrifice,—we must participate in His labors for their redemption."[1]

In fact, when the church fails to place priority on soul winning, it dies spiritually. "The very life of the church depends upon her faithfulness in fulfilling the Lord's commission. To neglect this work is surely to invite spiritual feebleness and decay. Where there is no active labor for others, love wanes, and faith grows dim."[2]

The great promise

Imagine what the disciples must have thought when Jesus told them to " 'go into all the world and preach the gospel to every creature' " (Mark 16:15)! The task must have seemed overwhelming, impossible to fulfill. How could such a small group make any impact on the mighty Roman Empire? Jesus' disciples must have wondered if it were even remotely possible for them to accomplish what Jesus had commissioned them to do.

Fortunately, this "Great Commission" is accompanied by a great promise. Before Jesus told His disciples to " 'make disciples of all the nations,' " He said, " 'all authority has been given to Me in heaven and on earth' " (Matthew 28:18, 19). The book of Acts tells us that just before He left, He also promised, " 'You shall receive power when the Holy Spirit has come upon you; and you shall be witnesses to Me in Jerusalem, and in all Judea and Samaria, and to the end of the earth' " (Acts 1:8). The Great Commission was to be accomplished only in Jesus' power. The disciples were to witness in His strength, not their own. They were to go forth *filled* with the Spirit, *empowered* by the Spirit, and *guided* by the Spirit. The Holy Spirit's presence and power in their lives would give them success.

What witnessing does

Prayer without a focus on witnessing can lead to self-centered fanaticism. Bible study without the outlet that witnessing provides can lead to self-righteous formalism. The Pharisees prayed and studied their Bibles for hours each day, but they condemned Jesus to death. Why? There is one simple reason. Their self-centered lives had little room for a selfless Messiah.

Witnessing starves selfishness to death. The fundamental purpose of prayer and Bible study is to draw us close to Jesus so He can entrust us with the power of the Holy Spirit. God won't pour out the latter rain to stroke our egos. He won't unleash it to transform complacent church members into passionate witnesses. It is the work of the early rain of the Spirit to convict us of sin, deepen our relationship with Jesus, strengthen us to face temptation, and reorder our priorities for witness. The later outpouring of the Spirit builds upon the foundation the early out-pouring has provided. It completes the work of God's grace in our lives and in the world.

We are counseled that "those only who are constantly receiving fresh supplies of grace, will have power proportionate to their daily need and their ability to use that power. . . . They are yielding them-selves daily to God, that He may make them vessels meet for His use. Daily they are improving the opportunities for service that lie within their reach. Daily they are witnessing for the Master wherever they may be."[3]

To be healthy, we must exercise regularly. When we neglect exercise, our immune system is weakened, and we become more susceptible to disease. Something similar happens to us spiritually when we don't exercise our faith through witnessing. Jesus' saying that " ' "it is more blessed to give than to receive" ' " works itself out in our spiritual lives (Acts 20:35). When we share God's Word with others, we grow spiri-tually. When we share our faith, it grows and becomes stronger.

Witnessing is the gentle breeze that fans the sparks of revival into pentecostal flames. When a revival of prayer and Bible study is not ac-companied by a life of witness and service, the flame will flicker out and the embers will soon become cold. When we don't witness, our spiritual experience degenerates into a cold, lifeless form. "It is in doing Christ's work that the church has the promise of His presence. . . . The very life of the church depends upon her faithfulness in fulfilling the Lord's commission. To neglect this work is surely to invite spiritual feebleness and decay. Where there is no active labor for others, love wanes, and faith grows dim."[4]

In the upper room, the disciples committed themselves to take the gospel to the world. They laid aside their personal agendas so they could focus their efforts on Christ's agenda. They surrendered their personal plans so they could carry out Christ's great plan. They surrendered their own ambitions so they could advance Christ's ambition to redeem the human race. One desire swallowed up all others: to fulfill Christ's commission by proclaiming the gospel to the world.

Imagine this scene

Scripture tells us what happened on earth in those days leading up to Jesus' ascension. Consider what the scene must have been when Jesus arrived in heaven. Ten thousand times ten thousand angels welcomed Him. The atmosphere was one of joy and celebration. The entire heavenly host sang that marvelous song of praise found in Revelation 5: " 'Worthy is the Lamb who was slain to receive power and riches and wisdom, and strength and honor and glory and blessing!' " (verse 12).

In my imagination, I see the mighty angel Gabriel approach Jesus. "Lord," he says, "You suffered much, dying for the sins of humankind. Your death provides eternal life for all who will accept it. Does everyone down on earth know that? Have they all heard of Your great sacrifice?"

"No, Gabriel, they haven't all heard," replies the Savior. "Just a handful of people in Jerusalem and Galilee know about it."

"Well, Master," continues Gabriel, "what is Your plan for informing everyone of Your great love?"

The Master replies, "I have commissioned My followers to carry the message of salvation to the entire world. I told them to tell others, who will in turn tell yet others, until the last person in the farthest corner has heard the story."

Gabriel's countenance changes. He sees what might be a flaw in the Master's plan, so he asks, "What if Peter grows weary of telling the story of the Cross and goes back to fishing? What if James and John and Andrew join him, and Matthew returns to his tax booth in Capernaum, and all the others lose their zeal and stop talking about Your sacrifice?

"Or what if these disciples die before the task is complete, and Your church grows large and comfortable, and the hearts of Your people no longer burn to tell the incredible story of Your love? What is Your backup plan?"

There is a long pause, and then we hear the voice of the Lord Jesus: "Gabriel, I have no other plan."

This scene, of course, is imaginary, but the lesson it teaches is true for every generation. Christ has given us the task, the privilege, of communicating the gospel to the people of this world. He has no other plan.

The father of modern missions

William Carey, the father of modern missions, was called by God to go to India when he was in his twenties. As the young pastor of a small Baptist church in Mouton, England, he attempted to persuade his superiors that they should engage in world evangelization. He was told, "Sit down, young man, and respect the opinions of your elders. If the Lord wants to convert the heathen, He will do it without your help."

But, as Carey recognized, Jesus has commissioned us to go. He hasn't told us that we can stay in the comfortable pews of our churches and criticize one another. We have a story to tell. A mission to accomplish. A message to share. And Christ has given us all we need to be able to share His truth in this crisis hour of earth's history. We go in His strength, not ours. We go with His authority. He supplies us with wisdom, strength, and courage.

Jesus has triumphed over the forces of evil. There is no situation too difficult for Him. When we accept His commission and witness for Him, we will see miracles, for He is the God of miracles. He will pour out His power through us. When "Christ gave His disciples their commission[,] He made full provision for the prosecution of the work, and took upon Himself the responsibility for its success. So long as they obeyed His word, and worked in connection with Him, they could not fail."[5]

Jesus will open doors for us too. When we share His love and truth with others, we go in His authority, with His power and His presence. He has declared, " 'I am with you always, even to the end of the age' " (Matthew 28:20). When you share Jesus with a colleague at work, Jesus is by your side. When you distribute literature from house to house, Jesus is with you. When you give Bible studies or direct some health or family life program, some youth or children's ministry, He is there to help.

An unforgettable scene

When I was a child, my father often took us from our home in southern Connecticut to New York City to visit the neighborhoods where he had lived as a child. Those places were in my father's blood, and he wanted his children to understand their heritage. His stories of growing up in the city were priceless family treasures—heirlooms to pass from one generation to the next.

An incident that occurred on one of those trips is as vivid in my mind today as it was when it happened more than forty years ago. In that time, sections of New York City's Bowery were havens for men and women who used liquor to escape the reality that they were living. The rundown tenement apartments, dingy bars, and trash-littered streets told the tragic story of shattered homes, broken bodies, and ruined lives.

The incident happened on a sweltering July day in the summer of 1968. As we waited for a traffic light to change, I gazed out the car window and thought about the lives of the unshaven, bleary-eyed men lying on the sidewalk in drunken stupors. Then I noticed that a red-faced man wearing a shabby plaid shirt was staggering toward us. When he got near, he said, "Could you spare a man a dollar?"

A dollar with which he could buy another drink? No!

But food? Yes!

We rummaged around and came up with a semblance of a lunch. As I handed it to him, he reached through the open window, cupped his hands around my head, and pulled my face toward his. The stench of alcohol on his breath was overpowering, but as I looked into those bloodshot blue-green eyes, he quietly said, "Thank You, Jesus," and then turned and staggered away.

Often since that day I have wondered, *If Jesus were here on our world today, where would He be? What would His priority be?*

The Bible leaves no doubt: Jesus' priority is people. Matthew's Gospel says, "Jesus went about all of the cities and villages, teaching in their synagogues, preaching the gospel of the kingdom, and healing every sickness and every disease among the people" (Matthew 9:35).

Jesus immersed Himself in the lives of people. He brought hope to the hopeless, peace to the troubled, forgiveness to the guilty, and power to the powerless. His heart overflowed with love for battered, bruised, and broken people.

Have you ever wept over the poverty of children who are not your own but who belong to Jesus? Has your heart ever ached as you've seen people who live hollow lives consumed with greed? Have you ever wept soul tears for the millions in the world's cities who are trying to eke out a meager existence but who question its meaning?

Listening to Jesus' heart

If we pause long enough, we may hear sobs—the heartbroken, agonizing cries of Jesus for lost people. "Our world is a vast lazar house, a scene of misery that we dare not allow even our thoughts to dwell upon. Did we realize it as it is, the burden would be too terrible. Yet God feels it all."[6] Scripture says, "In all their affliction He was afflicted" (Isaiah 63:9). Jesus experiences the pain of this world's sin in ways we can never imagine. Lost people are the object of His love. He longs for "all men to be saved and to come to knowledge of the truth" (1 Timothy 2:4). He is "not willing that any should perish but that all should come to repentance" (2 Peter 3:9).

If the burden of Jesus' heart isn't the burden of our hearts, are we really fully surrendered to Him? If we're complacent about sharing His love with lost people, can we really claim to be His disciples?

Ellen White said it well: "The church is God's appointed agency for the salvation of men. It was organized for service, and its mission is to carry the gospel to the world. From the beginning it has been God's plan that through His church shall be reflected to the world His fullness and His sufficiency. The members of the church, those whom He has called out of darkness into His marvelous light, are to show forth His glory."[7]

Our Lord's top priority is saving people, and there is no higher privilege or greater responsibility than participating with Him in His work of redeeming lost human beings.

Though the mission of sharing Jesus' love and truth with the entire world must have seemed overwhelming to His disciples, the results were astounding. The Christian church exploded in growth. Tens of thousands were converted. And the message of Jesus' love was carried to the remotest parts of the Roman Empire. In the year A.D. 110 or thereabouts, Pliny the Younger, governor of the Roman province of Bithynia, wrote to Emperor Trajan. He described what he was doing to find and execute Christians, and then he stated: "Many of every age, of every social class, even of both sexes, are being called to trial and will be called. Not cities alone but villages in even rural areas have been invaded by the infection of this superstition [Christianity]."[8]

Here we see that in the few generations that had passed since Jesus gave the gospel commission, Christianity had invaded nearly every level of society—even in Pliny's remote province. Ninety years later, Tertullian, a Roman lawyer turned Christian, wrote a defiant letter in defense of Christianity to the Roman magistrates. In it he stated that "nearly all the citizens of all the cities are Christians."[9]

The story of the book of Acts is the story of a revived church committed to witness for its Lord. Spiritual revival always leads to passionate witness. Sharing is the natural outgrowth of a transformed life. Jesus told His disciples, " 'Follow Me, and I will make you fishers of men' " (Matthew 4:19). The closer we follow Jesus, the more we will care about what He cares about. If we have little interest in sharing His love with others, maybe that's evidence that we're following Him at a distance and need revival.

Religious formalism leaves people spiritually barren, and doctrine alone won't transform hearts. The power of New Testament witnessing was rooted in the genuineness of lives changed by the gospel. The disciples weren't playacting. They weren't just going through the motions. Theirs was not some form of artificial spirituality. An encounter with the living Christ had changed them, and they couldn't remain silent.

Paul revealed what empowered New Testament witnessing. He said,

"The love of Christ compels us" (2 Corinthians 5:14). In other words, we are motivated, driven forward in our witness by the marvelous love of Jesus, which has changed our lives.

"Our confession of His faithfulness is Heaven's chosen agency for revealing Christ to the world. We are to acknowledge His grace as made known through the holy men of old; but that which will be most effectual is the testimony of our own experience. We are witnesses for God as we reveal in ourselves the working of a power that is divine."[10]

The most powerful witness is that given by a Christian who knows Jesus personally. There is no substitute for the testimony that springs naturally from a heart that is immersed in His love. Are you telling others about Jesus and what He's done for you?

---

1. Ellen G. White, *The Desire of Ages* (Nampa, Idaho: Pacific Press®, 1940), 142.
2. Ibid., 825.
3. White, *The Acts of the Apostles,* 55.
4. White, *The Desire of Ages,* 825.
5. Ibid., 822.
6. White, *Education,* 264.
7. White, *The Acts of the Apostles,* 9.
8. *Epistulae* 10.96.
9. *Apologeticus* 37.8.
10. White, *The Desire of Ages,* 347.

CHAPTER 5

Obedience: The Fruit of Revival

Confronted with the greatest challenge of His life, Jesus went to Gethsemane. He had visited this secluded olive grove that overlooked Jerusalem on numerous times before. There He could be alone. There He could pour out His soul to His heavenly Father. Away from the jostle and press of the crowds, He could enter into heartfelt communion with God.

On that night, which was fraught with eternal consequences, He fell on His face and cried out, " 'O My Father, if it is possible, let this cup pass from Me; nevertheless, not as I will, but as you will' " (Matthew 26:39). Recognizing the horrors that lay before Him, Jesus pled with the Father to remove the cup of sorrows He was about to drink. He wanted, if possible, to avoid Judas's betrayal, Pilate's judgment hall, the Roman lash, the crown of thorns, and the cross. Jesus didn't take the suffering He faced lightly. In Gethsemane, He fully realized that sin would crush out His life on Calvary's hill. But in the face of incredible physical, mental, and emotional anguish, Jesus chose to do the Father's will.

His prayer in Gethsemane revealed the guiding principle of His life: "Not My will, but Thy will be done." That principle was Jesus' life commandment. He was committed to doing the Father's will in every decision He made. Pleasing God was His motto. Obedience was the fruit of His relationship with God.

David described this single-minded focus of Jesus in a psalm. Speaking prophetically, he placed these words in the mouth of the Savior: " 'I delight to do Your will, O my God, and Your law is within my heart' " (Psalm 40:8). The writer of the book of Hebrews picks up the same refrain: " 'Then I said, "Behold, I have come—in the volume of the book it is written of Me—to do Your will, O God" ' " (Hebrews 10:7). The Holy Spirit brought Jesus' mind into conformity with His Father's will because Jesus had surrendered His own will and dedicated Himself to pleasing the Father in every aspect of His life. Jesus' life was a Spirit-filled life.

The Holy Spirit played a major role in every aspect of Jesus' life. Jesus was conceived of the Holy Spirit at birth and anointed with the Holy Spirit and power at baptism, when He began His public ministry (see Matthew 1:20; 3:16, 17; Acts 10:34–38). Throughout His life, Jesus obeyed His Father's will (John 8:29; Hebrews 10:7). The Spirit-filled life is an obedient life.

He who was "in the form" or very essence of God "made Himself," or as the original Greek text of the New Testament says, "emptied Himself" of His privileges and prerogatives as His Father's equal and became, as the original language says, "a bondservant [slave]" (Philippians 2:6, 7). The Master of all became a servant or slave to all.

To what was Jesus a slave? He voluntarily subordinated His will to the Father's will. He "humbled Himself" and "became obedient to the point of death, even the death of the cross" (verse 8).

Jesus shows us what kind of life human beings can have when they're filled with the Holy Spirit. Such a life is characterized by willing obedience and humble submission to the Father's will. And because those who live such lives are consumed with the passionate desire to see others saved in the Father's kingdom, their lives are devoted to prayer and service.

Obeying the Master's command

John Kenneth Galbraith was a Canadian-American economist whose books on economics were bestsellers from the 1950s through the 2000s.

Galbraith filled the role of public intellectual on matters of economics. Arguably, during his lifetime, he was the best-known economist in the world. He was awarded the Medal of Freedom in 1946 and the Presidential Medal of Freedom in 2000 for his contributions to our understanding of economics.

In his autobiography, *A Life in Our Times,* Galbraith related an incident that revealed the dedication of Emily Wilson, his family's housekeeper. "It had been a wearying day," he wrote, "and I asked Emily to hold all telephone calls while I had a nap. Shortly thereafter the phone rang. Lyndon Johnson was calling from the White House.

" 'Get me Ken Galbraith. This is Lyndon Johnson.'

" 'He is sleeping, Mr. President. He said not to disturb him.'

" 'Well, wake him up. I want to talk to him.'

" 'No, Mr. President. I work for him, not you,' Emily responded. When I called the president back [Galbraith wrote], he could scarcely control his pleasure. 'Tell that woman I want her here in the White House,' " Johnson said.[1]

Emily Wilson's unswerving loyalty to Kenneth Galbraith is very similar to the principled commitment Jesus was teaching His disciples in Gethsemane. However, it was in the upper room at Pentecost that the disciples really began to understand what Jesus was trying to teach them. "Like a procession, scene after scene of His wonderful life passed before them. As they meditated upon His pure, holy life they felt that no toil would be too hard, no sacrifice too great, if only they could bear witness in their lives to the loveliness of Christ's character."[2]

It was as the disciples sought God together in the upper room that they became totally committed to doing the Father's will. "Christ filled their thoughts; the advancement of His kingdom was their aim. In mind and character they had become like their Master, and men 'took knowledge of them, that they had been with Jesus.' Acts 4:13."[3]

Peter was a different man after Pentecost. He didn't tremble in fear at the accusations of the officers of the temple, as he would have before Pentecost. When these religious leaders confronted him and demanded that he stop preaching in Jesus' name, he responded, " 'We ought to obey God rather than men' " (Acts 5:29). Like his Master, Peter had but one overriding ambition: to do the will of his heavenly Father. This was true of each of the other Spirit-filled disciples too. They were willing to face persecution, imprisonment, and even death for Christ's sake.

Why?

They were passionate about doing Jesus' will. They had laid aside their own personal agendas. Knowing and obeying Jesus was now what they considered to be most important. Faith that leads to submission to Jesus' will has the highest priority in the life of every Christian. "The submission which Christ demands, the self-surrender of the will which admits truth in its sanctifying power, which trembles at the word of the Lord, are brought about by the work of the Holy Spirit. There must be a transformation of the entire being, heart, soul, and character. . . . Only at the altar of sacrifice, and from the hand of God, can the selfish, grasping man receive the celestial torch which reveals his own incompetence and leads him to submit to Christ's yoke, to learn His meekness and lowliness." [4]

Something remarkable happened in the upper room. The Holy Spirit brought deep conviction to each of the praying disciples. In the light of Jesus' eternal sacrifice on the cross, they recognized that their own commitment was superficial. They understood that God was calling for a much deeper consecration. Realizing the shallowness of their surrender to the cause of Christ, they opened their hearts to the Holy Spirit's working and committed their lives totally to doing God's will. God now had clear channels through which to pour His Holy Spirit.

If we will surrender ourselves totally to God's will, we also will be prepared to receive the full outpouring of the Holy Spirit. The latter rain will be poured out only upon those who have surrendered their hearts fully to God—to doing His will.

An example of instant obedience

Neil Marten, a well-known member of the British government, was giving a group of his constituents a guided tour of the Houses of Parliament. During the course of the visit, the group happened to meet Lord Hailsham, at that time Lord Chancellor of England. Lord Chancellor

Hailsham was wearing all the regalia of his office, and his royal garb made him look quite imposing.

Hailsham recognized Marten, his colleague and fellow parliamentarian, so he called out to him using his first name, "Neil!" At that, the entire group of visitors—not daring to question or disobey what they took to be a royal command—promptly dropped to their knees!

The visitors, of course, had confused the name *Neil* with the word *kneel*. But their instant obedience to a perceived command illustrates the point. They didn't hesitate or debate. Instead, they obeyed immediately.

Jesus was so committed to doing the Father's will that He accepted His commands without reservation. He invites us to do the same.

Is the Holy Spirit convicting you to surrender something right now? Is there something you cherish that God is calling you to give up? The same Holy Spirit who revives us will also empower us to do God's will.

Genuine revival always produces obedience. Revival's effects on the people who receive it can be seen in what happened in Wales during the years 1904–1906. Evan Roberts and his friends were in their late teens and early twenties during that time. They began to pray earnestly for the outpouring of the Holy Spirit. They interceded for others, studied Scripture, and shared their faith. And God answered their prayers and poured out the Spirit in abundance. In six months there were one hundred thousand conversions in the small country of Wales.

The results of this revival were seen throughout the country. Day and night people flocked to churches by the thousands for prayer. Rough, cursing coal miners were transformed into kind, courteous gentlemen. Drunkards became sober. Prostitutes became pure. Cheaters and thieves became honest. And the greedy donated money to help those in need. Even the ponies that worked in the coal mines were affected—they had to learn new commands because the miners were no longer using the old ones, which were filled with curses!

When people open their hearts to the Spirit's infilling, He never leaves them the same. He convicts them of sin, reveals the magnificence of a love that will not let them go, draws them to Jesus, and empowers them to live obedient lives.

Transformed lives

Sometimes the Bible writers felt extremely close to Jesus, and at other times they didn't. At times their spirits soared into ecstasy and they delighted in the joy of His presence. At other times they didn't feel Him near at all. But revival doesn't necessarily change how one feels. It changes what one does. Our feelings are not the fruit of revival—obedience is. This is evident in the lives of the disciples after Pentecost.

Consider Peter. The outpouring of the Holy Spirit on Pentecost made a dramatic difference in his life. It transformed him from a weak, vacillating disciple into a faith-filled, obedient one. Just before the Cross, the disciples were concerned about the position they would have in Jesus' new kingdom (Matthew 20:20–28). After Pentecost, their priorities were changed. They were focused on unselfish ministry to others. They now understood what Jesus meant when He said that if we help the people ranked lowest in society (people whom Jesus called His brothers and sisters), it's as if we've helped Him (Matthew 25:40). Filled with the Holy Spirit, they obeyed Jesus' command to " 'love one another as I have loved you' " (John 15:12). So, when the widows of some of the Greek converts were neglected in the daily distribution of food, the disciples didn't ignore them. They appointed deacons to meet their needs (Acts 6:1–7).

The infilling of the Holy Spirit led the disciples to care for the poor and disadvantaged. It led them to live unselfish, godly lives. It led them to obedience even though that obedience cost them a great deal. All but one of the disciples suffered a martyr's death. They were stoned, imprisoned, burned at the stake, shipwrecked, and more. Unusual power from above drew unusual power from beneath. At times the spiritual warfare was fierce, but Jesus, their Savior and Lord, was by their side to strength their faith.

The deacon Stephen is another example of a person whose life was transformed, which gave him a deep commitment to doing the Father's will. Acts 7 records the magnificent sermon he preached. In it he outlined the history of Israel and referred to the experiences of Abraham, Isaac, Jacob, Joseph, Moses, David, and Solomon, picturing God's faithfulness in contrast to Israel's unfaithfulness. Stephen concluded his sermon by charging that in rejecting Jesus, the religious leaders of the Israel of that day were violating God's covenant and resisting the influence of the Holy Spirit in the same way the Israel of old had rejected God's leading.

The infilling of the Holy Spirit led Stephen to minister unselfishly to the marginalized and disadvantaged widows. And it led him to obediently proclaim—in spite of the consequences to himself—the message of God's faithfulness to His chosen people and the rejection of that message by most of the religious leaders. Stephen's martyrdom is an eloquent testimony given by someone fully committed to doing God's will in spite of the consequences. Stephen was obedient to the call of God and faithful to the mission of God even when it meant giving his own life.

Sensitive to the Spirit's call

The Spirit-filled life is a changed life. The life of the apostle Paul illustrates this principle. Although Saul (Paul's original name) was misguided in his fierce persecution of Christians, he was honest. When he persecuted Christians, he thought he was doing God's will in confronting what he believed to be a fanatical sect.

As Saul journeyed to Damascus to capture Christians and drag them back to Jerusalem to stand trial, Jesus dramatically surprised him. Saul's Damascus Road experience changed not only his life, but also the world. That's where Saul the persecutor became Paul the evangelist. From that time on, his life was characterized by obedience to the Spirit's call. Paul preached with power throughout the Mediterranean world. He lit gospel fires in Galatia, Ephesus, Philippi, Colossae, and Thessalonica. His Spirit-filled ministry shook the Roman Empire— even, through his converts, reaching into Caesar's household (see Philippians 4:22; Colossians 1:23–29).

Throughout Paul's ministry, he was guided by the Spirit, convicted by the Spirit, instructed by the Spirit, and empowered by the Spirit. In his defense before King Agrippa, he described the heavenly vision that he saw while on the Damascus Road. He then testified that the purpose of his ministry to both Jews and Gentiles was " ' "to open their eyes, in order to turn them from darkness to light, and from the power of Satan to God, that they may receive forgiveness of sins and an inheritance among those who are sanctified by faith" ' " (Acts 26:18).

Paul's life indicates that to be filled with the Holy Spirit, one must respond to His convicting power. The Spirit doesn't fill hearts that are already filled with selfish desires. King Agrippa, for example, didn't yield to the convicting power of the Holy Spirit because his self-inflated importance and egotistical desires conflicted with the Spirit's prompting that he empty himself and live for Jesus.

The apostle Paul declares that Spirit-filled, New Testament believers have "received grace and apostleship for obedience to the faith among all nations for His name" (Romans 1:5). On the other hand, those who "are self-seeking and do not obey the truth, but obey unrighteousness" can expect to experience only "indignation and wrath" (Romans 2:8).

In these passages, the apostle Paul reveals that obedience is a matter of a surrendered heart. By faith we live for Jesus rather than for ourselves. By faith He is on the throne of our hearts, and self is on the cross. By faith we declare with Paul, "I have been crucified with Christ; it is no longer I who live, but Christ lives in me" (Galatians 2:20).

Though we are committed Christians, we still have struggles. We still experience temptations—Jesus certainly did too. We may stumble at times, but by grace we are still totally committed to doing God's will. Ellen White puts it beautifully in her book *The Acts of the Apostles:* "Those who at Pentecost were endued with power from on high, were not thereby freed from further temptation and trial. As they witnessed for truth and righteousness they were repeatedly assailed by the enemy of all truth, who sought to rob them of their Christian experience. They were compelled to strive with all their God-given powers to reach the measure of the stature of men and women in Christ Jesus. Daily they prayed for fresh supplies of grace, that they might reach higher and still higher toward perfection."[5]

The members of a country church were having their annual revival meetings. On the first night, the preacher delivered a message about repentance and the need to return to the Lord. When he made the altar call, a man came down the aisle, saying, "Fill me, Lord. Fill me."

The next night the preacher challenged the congregation with their need to surrender their lives to Christ in complete obedience. Again he extended the altar call, and the man who had responded the previous night came down the aisle a second time, saying, "Fill me, Lord. Fill me."

On the third night of the revival, the preacher warned his congregation of the evils of sin and urged them to live lives of holiness. And again, at the invitation to surrender to Christ, the now-familiar man came down the aisle, saying, "Fill me, Lord. Fill me." But this time, someone in the back of the church yelled, "Don't do it, Lord—he leaks!"[6]

The truth of the matter is that we all leak from time to time; we tend to lose our first love, or to wade in the pool of the lukewarm, or even to lose our way. But Jesus is there to strengthen, sustain, and support us. He is there to fill and empower us. He is there to patch the holes and fix the leaks. He is there to empower us to live obedient lives now and forever.

---

1. John Kenneth Galbraith, *A Life in Our Times* (Boston, Mass.: Houghton Mifflin, 1981), as quoted in *Reader's Digest,* December 1981.

2. Ellen G. White, *The Acts of the Apostles,* 36.

3. Ibid., 45.

4. White, *In Heavenly Places* (Hagerstown, Md.: Review and Herald®, 1995), 236.

5. White, *The Acts of the Apostles,* 49.

6. From a sermon, "Remember What We Are to Do," preached by Alan Tison on August 7, 2010.

CHAPTER 6

Confession and Repentance:
The Conditions of Revival

Imagine the disciples as members of a church board. How would you like to be the person who presided over the meetings of that board held before Pentecost? You would have had to contend with Peter's strong opinions, Thomas's doubts, and the outbursts of James and John, mingled with Matthew's exactness, Judas's selfishness, Andrew's introspection, and the prejudice of Simon the Zealot.

The revival at Pentecost made the difference. The Holy Spirit broke down the barriers between the disciples, and they tearfully repented and confessed their sins to God, and, where appropriate, to one another. And then warm, loving fellowship replaced the sharp divisions that had separated them.

Throughout Scripture, repentance and confession have opened the way for spiritual revival. God has always prepared His people to do a greater work for Him by leading them through godly sorrow for their failures. Repentance and confession are the necessary prerequisites to receiving the Spirit's power in abundance.

In this chapter, we will discover the nature of biblical repentance, contrast true repentance with false repentance, and trace the importance of true repentance as a prelude to the outpouring of the Holy

Spirit. And most important of all, we will discover that repentance is a gift that the Holy Spirit gives us to prepare us to reflect Jesus' love more clearly to those around us.

God's gift

Just before His ascension, Jesus gave the disciples the very specific instruction to "wait for the promise of the Father" (Acts 1:4). What did He mean? Were they simply to sit idly in that upper room in Jerusalem, or did they have a role to play in preparing their hearts to receive the heavenly gift? Was there something specific they needed to do? If so, what was it, and what does the disciples' upper room experience teach us about the outpouring of the Holy Spirit?

Ellen White gives us this divine insight regarding those ten days of waiting: "After Christ's ascension, the disciples were gathered together in one place to make humble supplication to God. And after ten days of heart searching and self-examination, the way was prepared for the Holy Spirit to enter the cleansed, consecrated soul temples."[1]

True repentance defined

The word *repentance* may evoke for you a range of feelings and mental images. What is genuine, biblical repentance? Is it characterized by overwhelming emotions so that it is always accompanied by sobbing and tears? Does it leave us depressed because of our guilt?

Repentance is a God-initiated sorrow for sin impressed upon our minds by the Holy Spirit. There are some very specific examples in the Bible of people who sought repentance but were not forgiven—see, for instance, the stories about Pharaoh, Balaam, Esau, and Judas (Exodus 12:29–32; Numbers 22:32–35; Hebrews 12:16, 17; and Matthew 27: 3, 4). These people weren't sorry about the sin itself. Nor were they sorry about the pain it brought to other people or to God. Their only concern was the consequences they were suffering because of their sin.

Hebrews 12:17 sums it up well. It says Esau repented "when he wanted to inherit the blessing." Esau wasn't concerned about the pain his sin brought to his family or to the heart of God. His only concern was that because of his sin he lost the birthright. He was sorry that he didn't get what he wanted. False repentance focuses on the consequences we suffer because of our sin. True repentance, however, grows out of the godly sorrow we feel because we have disappointed our Lord, because we've brought pain to the heart of the One who loves us with an everlasting love. So, sorrow that our sins have hurt other people and especially our Savior is an important characteristic of true repentance.

True repentance is also marked by an honest confession of the specific sins that we have committed. It isn't laced with excuses for the sinner's behavior. It doesn't place blame on someone else. Those who are truly repentant take responsibility for what they've done. (I'll say more about confession later in this chapter.)

True repentance doesn't stop with people's confession of their sins. It leads to their forsaking their sins, their turning away from the thoughts or words or actions that have broken God's heart. "Remorsefulness is sorry for the past, but doesn't want to change the future. Repentance is also sorry for the past, but makes a change in heart so the future will be different. It changes future behavior so the past mistakes won't be repeated."[2]

People who are truly repentant cry out with David, "Create in me a clean heart, O God, and renew a steadfast spirit within me. Do not cast me away from Your presence, and do not take Your Holy Spirit from me" (Psalm 51:10, 11). The longing of the truly repentant heart is a desire to please Jesus in every aspect of life.

Repentance that is genuine doesn't lead Christians into a state of deep depression because of their sinful natures or sinful deeds. "Godly sorrow produces repentance leading *to salvation*" (2 Corinthians 7:10; emphasis added). It leads us to focus on Jesus' righteousness, not on our sinfulness. It produces a diligence (verse 11) in "looking unto Jesus, the author and finisher of our faith" (Hebrews 12:2). Throughout the New Testament, our sin, though serious, never outweighs God's grace, for "where sin abounded, grace abounded much more" (Romans 5:20).

When the apostle Paul recognized that he was persecuting innocent people, children of the God he claimed to be serving, he was driven to his knees in genuine repentance and confession. But he wasn't left in a state of sorrow over his failures. His focus wasn't on how unrighteous he was; it was upon how righteous Jesus was.

We are instructed that we must lay our feelings "of guiltiness . . . at the foot of the cross of Calvary. The sense of sinfulness has poisoned the springs of life and of true happiness. Now Jesus says, 'Lay it all on Me. I will take your sins. I will give you peace. Banish no longer your self-respect, for I have bought you with the price of My own blood. You are mine. Your weakened will I will strengthen; your remorse for sin I will remove.' "[3]

True repentance is a gift. We can't genuinely repent of our sins unless we have received this gift from Jesus. Acts 5 pictures the apostles proclaiming the Jesus whom "God has exalted at His right hand to be prince and Savior, to give repentance to Israel and forgiveness of sins" (verse 31). It is the goodness of God that leads us to repentance (Romans 2:4). "We can no more repent without the Spirit of Christ to awaken the conscience than we can be pardoned without Christ.

"Christ is the source of every right impulse. He is the only one that can implant in the heart enmity against sin. Every desire for truth and purity, every conviction of our own sinfulness, is evidence that His Spirit is moving upon our hearts."[4]

Repentance and confession

As we have seen, repentance—this inner, God-given sorrow for sin—leads to the outer expression of our remorse in confession to God and to the people we have hurt by our words or actions. Genuine revival has always been accompanied by confession of sin. Confession opens the heart and clears the way for the Holy Spirit to fill us when God pours His Spirit upon the earth.

If the channels of our souls are clogged by sin, the Spirit cannot flow through us to the world. Unconfessed sin hinders what God desires to do through His church. The wise man stated, "He who covers his sins will not prosper, but whoever confesses and forsakes them will have mercy" (Proverbs 28:13). Before the Holy Spirit fills us and empowers us, He convicts us and instructs us. Unless we confess the sins the Holy Spirit points out, our hearts will become barren. If we refuse to listen to the Voice of conviction, we will never receive the outpouring of the Holy Spirit in latter-rain power.

As the disciples met in the upper room, earnestly seeking God in prayer, they clearly understood the need to confess their sins to God and, where appropriate, to one another. "After the ascension of Christ, the Holy Spirit did not immediately descend. There were ten days after His ascension before the Holy Spirit was given. This time was devoted by the disciples to most earnest preparation for receiving so precious an endowment. The rich treasures of heaven were poured out to them after they had searched their own hearts diligently and had sacrificed every idol. They were before God, humbling their souls, strengthening their faith, confessing their sins."[5]

There's a work of preparation that must be done before the outpouring of the Holy Spirit. Christ's disciples had walked with Him for three and a half years, yet they needed to spend time in prayer, meditation, repentance, and confession to prepare their hearts for the early rain that enabled them to launch the gospel proclamation in pentecostal power. How much more, then, do we need to prepare our hearts for earth's final, climactic hour? If sin blocked the mighty outpouring of the Holy Spirit in those days, then it certainly will do the same now. If confession prepared the hearts of the disciples to receive the Holy Spirit, it will prepare our hearts as well.

The Old Testament's sanctuary services provide vital lessons about the nature of confession. Leviticus 5 describes what happened when the Israelites had sinned and brought an offering to the sanctuary seeking forgiveness. Verse 5 says, " ' "It shall be, when he is guilty in any of these matters, that he shall confess that he has sinned in that thing." ' " The sinner who brought the lamb placed his hands upon its head and confessed the sin he had committed.

Genuine repentance leads to the confession of the specific sin the sinner has committed. "True confession is always of a specific character, and acknowledges particular sins. They may be of such a nature as to be brought before God only; they may be wrongs that should be confessed to individuals who have suffered injury through them; or they may be of a public character, and should then be as publicly confessed. But all confession should be definite and to the point, acknowledging the very sins of which you are guilty."[6]

The purpose of the convicting power of the Holy Spirit is to reveal our need of the saving grace of Christ. Repentance doesn't make God love us more; it enables us to appreciate His love more. Confession doesn't earn God's forgiveness; it enables us to receive the forgiveness that was in His heart all the time. God's love for us is constant. The problem is that we are totally incapable of receiving the abundant blessings God has for us while our spiritual arteries are clogged with the sludge of sin. Repentance and confession open the clogged channels of our spiritual hearts to receive the overflowing of the Holy Spirit's presence and power.

The sinner's psalm

In Psalm 51, we hear the cry of David's heart. This psalm reveals the depth of his pain. It is like an X-ray of his soul. David's repentance following his sin with Bathsheba was much more than a superficial, emotional feeling of sorrow. He recognized the shame that he had brought to the cause of God. He acknowledged the sorrow he had brought to God's heart. We become truly repentant when we recognize that our sin has brought pain to someone other than ourself. "The cross is a revelation to our dull senses of the pain that, from its very inception, sin has brought to the heart of God. Every departure from the right, every deed of cruelty, every failure of humanity to reach His ideal, brings grief to Him."[7] True repentance leads us to look upon the One whom we have pierced and mourn for Him just as a woman mourns for her only son (see Zechariah 12:10).

Confession is healing in many ways. It lances the boil of guilt and allows the poisonous puss of sin to drain. It opens our hearts to receive God's grace. Through confession we accept the forgiveness Christ offers us from Cross. At the Cross, all humanity was reconciled to God, but that reconciliation doesn't become effectual in our lives until we accept it by faith (Romans 5:10, 11, 17–19; Ephesians 2:1–10). Confession is healing because it allows us to receive grace, which is God's remedy for the sin problem. Confession also breaks down barriers between us and other people. It heals relationships.

Have you harbored critical thoughts? Have you spoken stinging, hurtful words? Have you been impatient or unkind? Have you been lax in keeping the Sabbath or unfaithful in returning tithe? Sin blocks the blessing God longs to pour out through us. Confession removes the blockage. As we kneel before our forgiving and merciful God, confessing the specific sins of which the Holy Spirit has convicted us, we will receive forgiveness and freedom from guilt and pardon.

Our consciences should clear as we confess our sins to God. The apostle Paul spoke of having a "conscience without offense toward God and men" (Acts 24:16). If after we have confessed our sins to God a sense of guilt still remains, we should ask ourselves whether we have wronged someone in any way. It may be that the Holy Spirit is prompting us to confess to them and to ask for their forgiveness.

Here's the primary principle for determining whether you should ask someone to forgive you. If you've broken a fence, you repair it. If your actions have created a rift in your relationship with another person, asking that person's forgiveness can mend that "broken fence." It can restore that relationship and testify of the power of God's grace working in your life.

There may be times when we feel guilty even though we have confessed our sins. Why? One reason might be that the devil is attempting to rob us of the assurance of salvation. He loves to steal away the blessed assurance of forgiveness and salvation we have in Jesus.

Clint, a new Christian, was attending an evangelistic series. The presentation on the second coming of Christ particularly impressed him. When the evangelist asked, "Is there anything in your life that would keep you from being ready for the coming of Jesus?" the Holy Spirit brought something specific to Clint's mind. Years before, he had been with a group of teenagers who had stolen things from a home in the community. So, Clint confessed his sin to God and claimed Christ's promise of forgiveness.

However, a few weeks later, Clint was still troubled by what he had done. When he told the evangelist what he was feeling, the evangelist explained that there are two kinds of guilt: moral guilt and psychological guilt. We experience moral guilt when we break God's law. We feel psychological guilt when we have wronged another person. Confessing sin to God takes away the moral guilt we have incurred, but we may continue to feel psychological guilt until we also confess the sin to the people we have wronged.

When Clint understood the need to ask forgiveness from, and if necessary make restitution to, the ones he had wronged, he immediately asked the evangelist to help him make things right. The evangelist contacted the family, and told them about Clint's confession and his desire for their forgiveness. When the evangelist told Clint that the family had said, "We forgive him," he broke down in tears. Now all his guilt was gone. All his burdens were lifted.

When is public confession appropriate? Public confession is appropriate when an individual has committed a public sin and brought disrepute on Christ and His church. If you have publicly turned away from your commitment to Christ and brought public rebuke on His name and the name of His church, public confession is appropriate. Although it is both unwise and unnecessary to go into all of the lurid details of the sin you have committed, a testimony of the sorrow you have felt because you disappointed God and despised His grace and of your intention now to serve Him will bring healing to your heart and to your church as well. At times, the Holy Spirit leads believers who have been separated by conflict that has become public to confess publicly. Here is the clear principle: The purpose of confession is reconciliation between the offender, the offended, and everyone else involved. The fence must be repaired where it is broken.

Jesus is the answer to our feelings of guilt. He is still the pardoning, forgiving Savior. He still cleanses us from the guilt and shame of sin. When we come and honestly confess our sins to Him, our hearts are prepared to receive the salvation He so freely offers and the empowerment of His Holy Spirit that He so freely gives.

A personal appeal

Is the Holy Spirit convicting you that there things in your life that are not in harmony with God's will? Do you have attitudes that aren't Christlike? Are you clinging to habits that you need to surrender? Are you willing to humble yourself before God in heartfelt repentance and ask Him to forgive you for your sinful attitudes?

> As you see the enormity of sin, as you see yourself as you really are, do not give up to despair. It was sinners that Christ came to save. We have not to reconcile God to us, but—O wondrous love!—God in Christ is "reconciling the world unto Himself." 2 Corinthians 5:19. He is wooing by His tender love the hearts of His erring children. No earthly parent could be as patient with the faults and mistakes of his children, as is God with those He seeks to save. No one could plead more tenderly with the transgressor. No human lips ever poured out more tender entreaties to the wanderer than does He. All His promises, His warnings, are but the breathing of unutterable love.[8]

When we come humbly before God in sincere confession and deep repentance, Jesus will say to us as He said to the thief who hung beside Him two thousand years ago, " 'Assuredly, I say to you today, you will be with Me in Paradise' " (Luke 23:43; punctuation modified). The good news is that through the grace of Christ, this assurance is ours today too.

1. Ellen G. White, *Evangelism,* 698.
2. Kent Crockett, *The 911 Handbook* (Peabody, Mass.: Hendrickson Publishers, 2003), 203.
3. White, *Manuscript Releases,* 9:305.
4. White, *Steps to Christ,* 26.
5. White, *This Day With God* (Washington, D.C.: Review and Herald®, 1979), 10.
6. White, *Steps to Christ,* 38.
7. White, *Education,* 263.
8. White, *Steps to Christ,* 35.

CHAPTER 7

Unity: The Bond of Revival

Years ago, Leslie Flynn penned a book titled *Great Church Fights*. In it he chronicled the way people went after each other—all the while saying that they were doing it in the name of Jesus Christ. Flynn tells of a man who heard a commotion in his backyard. He looked out a window and saw his daughter and several playmates quarreling heatedly with each other. When the man intervened, his daughter exclaimed, "Dad, we're just playing church!"

Where jealousy, envy, and jostling for supremacy reign, the power of God wanes. How crucial then that we learn how to break down the barriers that sometimes separate us. Jesus' desire was that we enter into the unity for which He prayed in the great intercessory prayer recorded in John 17. While He was interceding earnestly for His disciples, His prayer was for us too. It echoes down the corridors of time and speaks to His church in all ages.

As Jesus prepared to leave His disciples, the unity of His church was on His mind. Soon He would be betrayed and crucified, and then He would rise from the grave and ascend to His Father. Jesus' earnest prayer reveals what was important to Him just before His cruel death on Calvary's cross. His prayer then is His prayer now. He said, " 'My prayer is not for them [His first-century disciples] alone. I pray also for those who will believe in me through their message, that all of them may be one, Father, just as you are in me and I am in you. May they also be in us so that the world may believe that you have sent me. I have given them the glory that you gave me, that they may be one as we are one' " (John 17:20–22, NIV).

Jesus' prayer clearly tells us that the unity of the church was His top priority. He knew that this unity was essential if the mission He was soon to give the church was to be accomplished. Jesus' longing was that the dissension, jealousy, striving for supremacy, and conflict between His disciples cease. He prayed that in spite of all their differences, they would have a unity that would reveal to the world the power of His love.

Many years ago, I was invited to conduct a Week of Spiritual Emphasis at a Christian school. As the week progressed, it became obvious to me that two of the teachers were having a serious conflict. Their negative attitudes toward one another regularly boiled over in staff meetings. If one suggested an idea, the other opposed it.

Toward the end of the week, I preached on Jesus' intercessory prayer. And the last night we met, we celebrated the ordinance of humility and the Lord's Supper. During those services, the Holy Spirit broke through. The two teachers who experienced such division washed one another's feet, and then they embraced, confessed their negative attitudes, and prayed together. The Holy Spirit changed their hearts, and the school environment soon reflected this amazing change.

Proud hearts are not new. Before Pentecost, selfish ambition reigned among the disciples. James and John urged their mother to petition Jesus to give them each a prominent place in the earthly kingdom they believed He was about to establish. (See Matthew 20.) This, of course, aroused suspicion and jealousy among the other disciples, and none of them were ready for the outpouring of the Holy Spirit. It was because of this that Jesus sent the disciples to the upper room and kept them there praying together for ten days. Before the Holy Spirit could fill them, they must be united.

Christ's prayer for His church and its leaders was answered. The disciples surrendered their differences and banished strife, and love prevailed. In the rest of the book of Acts, Luke pictures the unity of these first-century believers. Acts says that the disciples were "with one accord" (Acts 1:14; 2:1, 46).

One accord

Revivalist A. W. Tozer shares a fascinating illustration about what it means to be in "one accord." He says, "Has it ever occurred to you that one hundred pianos all tuned to the same fork are automatically tuned to each other? They are of one accord by being tuned, not to each other, but to another standard to which each one must individually bow. So one hundred worshippers meeting together, each one looking away to Christ, are in heart nearer to each other than they could possibly be were they to become 'unity' conscious and turn their eyes away from God to strive for closer fellowship. Social religion is perfected when private religion is purified."[1]

The closer we draw to Jesus, the closer we draw to one another. The Spirit of Christ enables us to see everything—including each other— with new spiritual eyesight. The grace of Christ reframes the little things that once bothered us. In the light of His magnificent grace, we relinquish cherished hostilities. We set aside scores that we once felt must be settled. Barriers are broken down. The gospel heals broken relationships.

When the Holy Spirit was poured out in its fullness on Pentecost, the attitudes of the disciples toward one another were dramatically changed. In the light streaming from the Cross, they saw one another differently. "Every Christian saw in his brother a revelation of divine love and benevolence. One interest prevailed; one subject of emulation swallowed up all others. The ambition of the believers was to reveal the likeness of Christ's character and to labor for the enlargement of His kingdom."[2]

As the New Testament believers sought God in prayer, the Holy Spirit knit their hearts together in Christian love. Luke recorded in the book of Acts, "These all continued with one accord in prayer and supplication, with the women and Mary the mother of Jesus, and with His brothers" (Acts 1:14). The record continues in Acts 2:1. "When the Day of Pentecost had fully come, they were all with one accord in one place." Ellen White adds, "Notice that it was after the disciples had come into perfect unity, when they were no longer striving for the highest place, that the Spirit was poured out. . . .

"The disciples did not ask for a blessing for themselves. They were weighted with the burden of souls. The gospel was to be carried to the ends of the earth, and they claimed the endowment of power that Christ had promised. Then it was that the Holy Spirit was poured out, and thousands were converted in a day."[3]

During those ten days in the upper room, the disciples confessed their petty differences toward one another. The barriers between them crumbled; they repented of their jealousy and pride; and their hearts were filled with love for the Christ who gave His life for them and who now was at the Father's right hand, interceding in their behalf. Their selfish ambitions were swallowed up in their love for Christ. The disciples learned through their experience that "unity with Christ establishes a bond of unity with one another. This unity is the most convincing proof to the world of the majesty and virtue of Christ, and of His power to take away sin."[4] Genuine conversion results in unity in the home and in the church, because "those who are truly converted will press together in Christian unity."[5]

The fourth chapter of Acts records how our relationships with Christ and with one another affect our witnessing. Luke wrote, "The multitude of those who believed were of one heart and one soul; neither did anyone say that any of the things he possessed was his own, but they had all things in common. And with great power the apostles gave witness to the resurrection of the Lord Jesus. And great grace was upon them all" (Acts 4:32, 33). This passage links the disciples' having "one heart and one soul" with their "great power" in witnessing. In the challenging circumstances of first-century Jerusalem, living at a time when Christianity was unpopular, these committed Christians shared their resources. They laid aside their ambitions and supported one another. Their unselfish attitudes and generosity of spirit prepared them to receive the fullness of the Holy Spirit's power for witnessing. Barriers between church members are also barriers to the reception of the Holy Spirit's power. Conflict between members of the church creates logjams, blocking the rivers of the Spirit's blessing. How important then that we put aside our petty differences so Jesus' intercessory prayer can be fulfilled in us and through us.

Foundations of unity

Christian unity rests upon the foundation of the spiritual things we share.

All of us have the same Father. We are one by virtue of the fact that He made us all. Scripture says He has made of *one blood* all nations (Acts 17:26).

All of us have the same Redeemer. We are one by virtue of the fact that all of the redeemed have been redeemed by God (Ephesians 2:14–22).

All of us have the same heritage. All who belong to Christ are part of His body, and God has gifted all of us for service. Some have greater gifts than others, but every believer has at least one gift that is valuable for building up the body of Christ (1 Corinthians 12:4–11, 18–21).

All of us have been called by God to the same mission. All of us have been commissioned to deliver a message to the world.

Former pastor Eric Daniel Harris pled guilty to the arson that burned down the Kentucky Missionary Baptist Church in Saline County, Arkansas—his church. According to a federal prosecutor, Harris said he did it because "there was a division among church members, and they needed a project to unify them."[6]

What Harris did was unthinkable for a Christian pastor. Certainly, his act was both strange and criminal, but in a bizarre way it does illustrate the point. Something that hits the church hard, that calls for major commitments on the part of the members, does unite them. But the replacement of their building was an artificial need; Christ has given us a greater goal—bringing the lost people in the communities where we live to Christ. Mission is the answer to the church's lethargy. Sharing the gospel with the world fans both the flames of unity and revival.

The disciples were united because Jesus gave all of them the same task—that of delivering a message they all shared to a world that hadn't heard. All of us, too, are united through having been commissioned to carry a special end-time message that is to prepare this world for the return of our Lord (Ephesians 4:12, 13; Revelation 14:6–12).

All of us have been given the same message to give to the world. The New Testament church was united in its message. The disciples preached the centrality of Christ (Colossians 1:19–23). Christ and Him crucified was their message (1 Corinthians 1:21–23). They were clear that " 'there is no other name under heaven given among men by which we must be saved' " (Acts 4:12). The life, death, resurrection, priestly ministry, and return of our Lord bound them together. New converts were anchored in the "apostles' doctrine" (Acts 2:41, 42). Their unity was founded upon the teachings of Jesus—what the apostle Peter termed "present truth" (2 Peter 1:12). This present truth united the church and motivated it.

Now, in the final days of earth's history, God has again given His people an urgent, present-truth message. It is this message that provides the foundation upon which the unity of God's modern-day people rests. This "everlasting gospel" of Christ's redeeming love and grace in the setting of the three angels restores the truth of the Sabbath in the context of the second coming of Jesus (Revelation 14:6–12). If the message that unites us—the message of the three angels—is watered down, pushed into a secondary place, or treated as a relic of the nineteenth century, the unity of the church will be fractured. The mission of the church will lose its urgency. The message of the church will become murky and unclear, and we will lose our reason for existence as a prophetic, end-time movement. It is the proclamation of the prophetic message of the three angels that justifies the Seventh-day Adventist Church's existence.

All of us belong to the same church. Seventh-day Adventists around the world are united by a single church organization and structure. Seventeen million Seventh-day Adventists spread throughout more than two hundred countries study the same Sabbath School Bible study guides, give to the same mission projects, support the same worldwide work with their tithes and offerings, participate in the election of world leaders every five years, and have similar administrative structures in conferences, unions, divisions, and the General Conference. The similar organization of the church throughout the world contributes to the unity of the worldwide Seventh-day Adventist Church.

So, the New Testament followers of Jesus all had the same Creator, the same Redeemer, the same heritage, the same mission, the same message, and the same structure. The believers of today do too. The things that unite us are far more numerous than all that seems to divide us.

Structure and unity

The New Testament world was to a large degree divided by caste, social status, gender, and age. It was a world in turmoil. The concepts of equal rights, democratic forms of government, and human dignity were foreign to most people. When Christianity stepped into the scene, it created a social revolution. Jesus' teachings of equality, justice, concern for the poor, and respect for the marginalized were considered radical in that day.

In a world still characterized by fractured relationships, power struggles, and divisive schisms, this bond of loving unity is still a powerful argument for Christianity. Jesus stated this universal truth clearly: " 'By this all will know that you are My disciples, if you have love for one another' " (John 13:34, 35). The members of the New Testament church revealed the power of the gospel in their lives. In spite of their differences, they were united in Jesus' love, and His Holy Spirit marvelously blessed their witness and ministry.

Is Christian unity, then, entirely a "spiritual" matter? To the surprise of many, a careful study of the New Testament reveals that the early church had a definite organizational structure. This structure helped preserve the doctrinal purity of the church and kept it focused on mission. In Acts 6, a small group of disciples met together to solve the problem of the distribution of food to the widows of the Greek converts. They selected deacons to solve the problem, and the church respected the authority of these church leaders.

When the apostle Paul was converted on the Damascus Road, he was directed to Ananias, a representative of the church (Acts 9:10–17). After Paul's baptism by Ananias, the Holy Spirit directed him to meet with the leaders of the church in Jerusalem, who would then confirm his ministry (verses 26–30). Acts 20 indicates that later in his life, Paul met with the elders of the church in Ephesus and urged them to be on guard against false teachers who would try to enter the church and spread their heresies (Acts 20:17, 27–32).

Acts also tells us that the Jerusalem council saved the first-century church from a serious schism. The leaders of the church with the administrative authority granted them served the New Testament church by preserving its doctrinal integrity. In this instance, representatives of the various congregations went to Jerusalem to participate in important doctrinal discussions. When the members of this representative committee came to a consensus, they wrote out their decision and circulated it throughout the churches where the problem had originated (Acts 15:23). The church membership accepted the decision of the Jerusalem council and rejoiced that the Holy Spirit had guided them to an answer to their dilemma (verses 30–35).

The unity and structure of the New Testament Christian church provided a climate that supported revival. Church leaders traveled to the congregations, sharing a message of revival. New churches were established, and those that already existed were strengthened and stabilized. The organizational structure of the New Testament church preserved its unity, and organization preserves the unity of the church today.

God longs to reveal His love to the world through His church. His intent is that "the manifold wisdom of God might be known by the church to the principalities and powers in the heavenly places, according to the eternal purpose which He accomplished in Christ Jesus our Lord" (Ephesians 3:10, 11).

Unity is not achieved by hoping or wishing for it. It is the by-product of something much larger. The Acts account reveals three basic practices that kept the believers who lived during the New Testament era united. They prayed together. They studied God's Word together. And together they worked to share their faith.

Prayer, Bible study, and witness are powerful elements for creating, fostering, and sustaining the unity of the church. As we pray with and for one another, we are drawn closer together. Studying with each other the exhaustless love and grace of God as revealed in His Word fills our hearts with love for one another. And participating in evangelistic outreach to the community in which we live creates a sense of oneness or togetherness. Depending on God to work a miracle of His grace to reach our friends and neighbors with the gospel brings us together.

A living, dynamic, unified, revived church is one in which the members are praying together, studying God's Word together, and reaching out to their community together. This is heaven's plan for your church. This is God's purpose for your congregation. Anything less falls short of His divine ideal and limits the effectiveness of His people—His messengers.

Church conflicts are a mockery of the gospel. Arguing with one another in the name of Jesus is contrary to the spirit of Christianity. Friction destroys fellowship. Thank God, there is a solution. Praying together with humble hearts, confessing our sins, repenting of our pride, and interceding for one another and a lost world still unites hearts—even those separated by a seemingly uncrossable chasm.

---

1. A. W. Tozer, quoted in "Unity," The Quotable Christian, accessed March 27, 2013, http://www.pietyhilldesign.com/gcq/quotepages/unity.

2. Ellen G. White, *The Acts of the Apostles,* 48.

3. White, *Counsels for the Church,* 98.

4. White, *The Seventh-day Adventist Bible Commentary,* 5:1148.

5. White, *Gospel Workers,* 485.

6. "News of the Weird," March 30, 2000.

CHAPTER 8

Discernment: The Safeguard of Revival

One day early in my ministry, I was studying the Bible with a family when a gruff old man who was smoking a big cigar walked into the room and fairly shouted, "Praise the Lord, I'm healed!" When I asked what disease he'd had, he exclaimed, "Cancer!" I was amazed. Here he was, claiming that God had healed him of lung cancer, and all the while he was puffing away on a cigar!

Do you think God would extend a man's life just so he could intentionally harm his body? It seems, then, that Satan was misleading the poor man.

Some of Satan's deceptions are more sophisticated. When I was teaching a prophecy seminar titled "Unsealing Daniel's Mysteries," a middle-aged woman approached me after an evening's presentation with amazement written all over her face. As she drew near, she blurted out, "Pastor, thank you so much for tonight's class. You've given me hope!"

This woman said that about six months earlier she had been diagnosed with cancer, and since then the cancer had metastasized. Her future looked ominous. She said that some well-meaning Christian friends told her that if she had enough faith, God would heal her. So she prayed; but instead of getting better, she got worse.

Her friends then said she must have some sin in her life that kept God from healing her. The woman told me that this assertion devastated her. Now, not only did she have cancer, but she'd also been pronounced faithless and guilty of harboring some secret sin.

"But now," the woman said, "I understand faith for the first time. Having faith doesn't mean that I have the confidence in myself to demand that God give me what I want. It means trusting in every circumstance of my life that He's still my best Friend. It means knowing that He wishes me no harm and that He always has my best interest in view even if I don't understand His ways."

The cigar man demanded that God heal him; the cancer-ridden woman trusted God even though He didn't heal her. The cigar man claimed to be healed; she was at peace even though she wasn't healed. Spiritual discernment leads us to accept God's ways even when we don't understand them. It leads us to a "peace that passes understanding" and a trust that at times defies human reason.

Counterfeit faith is self-centered. It focuses on our will, not God's; our desires, not His; what we want, not what He wants. This self-centered attitude makes us vulnerable to satanic delusions. Genuine biblical faith, on the other hand, is not based on our feelings, our logic, or the circumstances of our lives. Instead, it is God centered. It focuses on His unconditional love, His personal concern, and His almighty power.

Can the devil create false religious excitement, perform counterfeit miracles, and leave the impression that a genuine revival has occurred? The answer, of course, is Yes. At times, Satan works under the guise of false revivals, signs, and wonders. However, the answer to the problem of false revivals is certainly not the opposite extreme—cold religious formalism. Neither is it lukewarm Laodiceanism. God can and does work miracles, and we should expect more of them as history races toward a climax. In this chapter, we will study the indicators of genuine revival as well as obvious signs of false revivals. Knowing the difference between the two will save us from the enemy's delusions.

God's will and His Word

The essence of true revival is discovering and doing God's will as communicated through His Word. Consider the revival in the days of Josiah, king of Judah. During the reigns of Manasseh and Amon, Judah had turned far from God's Word and His will, losing most if not all of the blessings that they had received from the Spirit-led revival that the nation had experienced when Hezekiah ruled. Josiah was determined to lead God's people back to obedience to His will.

Hilkiah, the high priest, " 'found the Book of the Law in the house of the LORD' " (2 Kings 22:8). We're told that when this portion of Scripture was read to King Josiah and his subjects, they repented and sought God in prayer. Then they destroyed their idols and expelled from Judah the idolatrous priests and the spiritualist mediums. The Holy Spirit worked through the Word to begin a nationwide spiritual renewal and reformation.

The aims of all true spirituality are to know God and to do His will. (See John 17:3; Hebrews 10:7.) Any so-called revival that focuses on our experience rather than God's will and His Word misses the mark completely. The Holy Spirit would never lead us onto paths God's Word forbids us to take. The same Holy Spirit who inspired the Word leads us to the Word in the great decisions of our lives (2 Timothy 3:15, 16). The Word of God is both the foundation and the heart of all true revival.

Jesus declared, " 'It is the Spirit who gives life; the flesh profits nothing. The words that I speak to you are spirit, and they are life' " (John 6:63). Jesus' statement has great significance. The Holy Spirit, who is the Source of all spiritual revival, speaks through God's Word, giving genuine spiritual life to those who follow His guidance. Revival occurs when the Holy Spirit impresses Jesus' words upon our minds. This is why the Savior said, " ' "Man shall not live by bread alone, but by every word that proceeds from the mouth of God" ' " (Matthew 4:4). When people neglect or downplay the Word of God, they set the stage for a false revival characterized by religious excitement. Ellen White gives us this solemn warning:

In many of the revivals which have occurred during the last half century, the same influences have been at work, to a greater or less degree, that will be manifest in the more extensive movements of the future. There is an emotional excitement, a mingling of the true with the false, that is well adapted to mislead. Yet none need be deceived. In the light of God's Word it is not difficult to determine the nature of these movements. Wherever men neglect the testimony of the Bible, turning away from those plain, soul-testing truths which require self-denial and renunciation of the world, there we may be sure that God's blessing is not bestowed.[1]

In our time, too, God's Word is the very foundation of revival and a safeguard against the deceptions of the enemy. So, we are instructed that "none but those who have fortified the mind with the truths of the Bible will stand through the last great conflict."[2]

God's love and His law

Knowing Jesus—really knowing Him as a Friend—is the essence of all revival. The apostle Paul told the Ephesians that he was praying for them "to know the love of Christ which passes knowledge; that you may be filled with all the fullness of God" (Ephesians 3:19). Jesus Himself spoke of this relationship. In His parable of the ten virgins, five run out of oil. When they obtain some and ask if they can now join the wedding celebration, the Bridegroom, Jesus, tells them, " ' "I do not know you" ' " (Matthew 25:12).

Outwardly, those five virgins seemed to have a form of godliness, but they lacked an intimate experience with Jesus. He put His finger on the very heart of the Christian faith when He prayed, " 'This is eternal life, that they may know You, the only true God, and Jesus Christ whom You have sent' " (John 17:3). Jesus' greatest longing is to have close, personal fellowship with the people who comprise His last-day church (Revelation 3:20).

In every generation, the devil has attempted to counterfeit true revival and introduce falsehoods. Evidently, in John's day, under the guise of revival, some forms of heresy infiltrated the church. There were, for instance, Christian Gnostics who mingled nonbiblical teachings with the truths of God's Word. They denied the Incarnation, teaching that Jesus only *seemed* to have a human body, and they taught that the way to be saved is to learn the esoteric "truths" that only they could teach.

John countered these heretics by focusing on Jesus' birth, death, and resurrection and by setting forth the reality that "knowing God" in the spiritually effective sense means much more than knowing things God supposedly has hidden from other people. The knowledge of God that counts is what people learn through having a personal relationship with Him. For John, knowing Jesus meant experiencing His grace personally, loving Him supremely, and obeying Him wholeheartedly.

John highlighted his understanding of what it means to know Jesus in these words: "He who says he abides in Him ought himself also to walk just as He walked" (1 John 2:6). In the Greek original of this text, the word translated as "abide" is *meno.* It means to continue to be present or to remain, pointing us toward a continual abiding or remaining in Jesus' presence, which then leads us to a transformed life, a life of obedience. Experiencing Jesus' love, meditating upon His immense sacrifice, and contemplating the Cross and how much Jesus has done for us changes us. At the Cross our hard hearts are broken, and we are made new in the light of His overwhelming sacrifice.

In his book *Miracle on the River Kwai,* Ernest Gordon tells an amazing story about the power of sacrificial love. The events took place in a World War II prisoner-of-war camp in western Thailand. The soldiers held there were put to work on a railroad bridge. The conditions of their captivity were so bad that their behavior had become barbarous—they were abusing each other. Then one afternoon something happened that changed their lives.

The captors held the prisoners accountable for the tools they were using, counting them frequently to make sure that none were stolen. At one of these "tool counts," the guards came up one shovel short. Gordon wrote,

The officer in charge became enraged. He demanded that the missing shovel be produced, or else. When nobody in the squadron budged, the officer got his gun and threatened to kill them all on the spot. . . . It was obvious the officer meant what he had said. Then, finally, one man stepped forward. The officer put away his gun, picked up a shovel, and beat the man to death. When it was over, the survivors picked up the bloody corpse and carried it with them to the second tool check. This time, no shovel was missing. Indeed, there had been a miscount at the first check point.

The word spread like wildfire through the whole camp. An innocent man had been willing to die to save the others! . . . The incident had a profound effect. . . . The men began to treat each other like brothers.

When the victorious Allies swept in, the survivors, human skeletons, lined up in front of their Japanese captors and instead of attacking them insisted: "No more hatred. No more killing. Now what we need is forgiveness."

Love—sacrificial love—makes a profound difference. The heart of all true revival is a heartfelt appreciation for the unconditional, all-encompassing, sacrificial love of Jesus.

Formalism, fanaticism, and faith

One of the challenges of true revival is avoiding the extremes—breaking through icy formalism while staying away from the flames of fanaticism.

Formalists are rigidly locked into the status quo. They are satisfied with the external husks of religion while denying faith's living reality. Fanaticists stand at the other extreme. They tend to focus on one aspect of faith to the neglect of all others, and often they are self-righteous and judgmental. Both formalism and fanaticism are foes of genuine, biblical faith. Such a faith breaks their stranglehold. It is the hand that reaches out to receive the power of the Holy Spirit in Revelation's promised last-day revival.

Jesus saved some of His most scathing rebukes for religious leaders who were merely pretending to be religious while their hearts were filled with selfishness and greed. He exclaimed, " 'Woe to you, scribes and Pharisees, hypocrites! For you pay tithe of mint and anise and cummin, and have neglected the weightier matters of the law: justice and mercy and faith. These you ought to have done, without leaving the others undone' " (Matthew 23:23).

The Greek word *hypokrisis* is the root of our English word *hypocrite*. It means "play acting" or "to play a part." Dictionary.com defines it as "having a pretense of a virtuous character, moral or religious beliefs or principles that one does not really possess." The problem with religious formalism is that it has all the outer trappings of spirituality, but it lacks a transformed heart. Icy formalism needs to be warmed by the fires of revival so its coldness melts in the glory of God's presence.

Fiery fanaticism is equally dangerous. Signs and wonders can never take the place of authentic biblical faith. They are not a substitute for surrendering to the will and Word of God. The essence of real revival is a faith in Jesus that is so deep that it leads people to commit themselves to do His will. A biblically based revival echoes John's words: "Whatever is born of God overcomes the world. And this is the victory that has overcome the world—our faith" (1 John 5:4). Ellen White asked, "What kind of faith is it that overcomes the world? It is that faith which makes Christ your own personal Savior—that faith which, recognizing your helplessness, your utter inability to save yourself, takes hold of the Helper who is mighty to save, as your only hope."[3]

Ministry and miracles

The people involved in false revivals often place their major emphasis on spectacular signs and wonders. Genuine revivals focus instead on ministry and self-sacrificial service. They recognize that the greatest miracle is a changed life.

The healing miracles of Jesus testified to the fact that He is the Messiah. As our compassionate Redeemer, the Savior was concerned about alleviating human suffering, but He was even more concerned about the eternal salvation of everyone He touched with His healing grace.

The purpose of Jesus' ministry was " 'to seek and to save' " lost humankind (Luke 19:10).

Jesus used His healing of the paralytic to prove His spiritual power and authority. He told the Jewish religious leaders that He was about to perform a miracle so that " 'you may know that the Son of Man has power on earth to forgive sins.' " Then He told the paralytic to " 'arise, take up your bed, and go to your house' " (Matthew 9:6). The crowds who saw this miracle glorified God (verse 8). Miracles revealed God's love to all humanity and gave credibility to Jesus' redemptive ministry. He didn't come to earth primarily for the purpose of performing miracles. He wasn't some sensational wonder worker. He was the world's Redeemer (John 3:16; Matthew 1:21).

Jesus taught, preached, and healed for one distinct purpose—to glorify His heavenly Father. His earthly ministry revealed the Father's love and care. At the pool of Bethesda, Jesus healed a hopeless sufferer who had lain at the water's edge for thirty-eight years. After Jesus healed the man, He warned him to " 'sin no more, lest a worse thing come upon you' " (John 5:14). Jesus' miracles were always performed in the context of His larger ministry—glorifying His heavenly Father and making obedient disciples.

The apostle Paul outlined the end-time strategy of the "lawless one" (the antichrist). He said that evil power would work with "all power, signs, and lying wonders" (2 Thessalonians 2:9). Jesus also warned His disciples about the cunning devices of the evil one. He declared that " 'false christs and false prophets will rise and show great signs and wonders to deceive, if possible, even the elect' " (Matthew 24:24). Revelation confirms this stark reality: Satan will use miracles to deceive multitudes and lead them to receive the mark of the beast. (See Revelation 13:13, 14; 16:14; 19:20.) Note carefully why millions will be deceived by these false miracles. It is "because they did not receive the love of the truth, that they might be saved," and since they "did not believe the truth but had pleasure in unrighteousness," they accepted a strong delusion and believed a lie (2 Thessalonians 2:10–12). Paul makes a fascinating point. He says these people will be deceived by false miracles *because they did not receive the love of the truth.* When people desire the spectacular more than they do the life-changing truths of God's Word, their minds are open to deception.

The parable of the rich man and Lazarus concludes with Jesus' insightful words. " 'He [God] said to him, "If they do not hear Moses and the prophets, neither will they be persuaded if one rise from the dead" ' " (Luke 16:31). In other words, spectacular signs and marvelous wonders can never take the place of understanding and following God's Word. Obedience to God is primary. Miracles are supernatural events in which God works to alleviate suffering, bring glory to His name, and give credibility to the proclamation of the gospel. God never intended that they be a substitute for doing His will.

Mature Christians seek to know Jesus intimately. Their relationship with Him is vital. They are willing to allow Him to work through them in the ways He sees best. They seek to live godly, obedient lives, and they let Him impart the gifts that will best equip them to serve Him. They recognize that the fruits of the Spirit are the hallmarks of genuine revival.

---

1. Ellen G. White, *The Great Controversy*, 464.
2. Ibid., 593.
3. White, *Reflecting Christ* (Washington, D.C.: Review and Herald®, 1985), 21.

CHAPTER 9

Reformation: The Outgrowth of Revival

Recently, a colleague and I were discussing the church's renewed emphasis on revival and reformation, and he asked, "What precisely do we mean by the term *reformation*?"

His reason for raising the question was certainly valid. *Reformation* can mean different things to different people. Are we speaking of the religious reform movement in the sixteenth century? Or are we talking about the "Reform Adventists," who believe the church is fallen and that God has called them to come out of the church to form a separate movement. Or do we have in mind diet and dress reform? Is *reformation* about changing our medical and educational institutions? Does it necessarily mean that the church is in apostasy?

Revival and reformation are nothing new. They both should be ongoing experiences in the life of every believer. Since our natures are fallen, the Holy Spirit leads us to spiritual renewal every day. Daily, God pours fresh supplies of His grace and power on those who kneel before His throne. When we spend time in His glorious presence through prayer and the study of His Word, we are changed. Perhaps that's why the psalmist cried out, "I am afflicted very much; revive me, O LORD, according to Your word" (Psalm 119:107).

In his second letter to the Thessalonians, the apostle Paul calls it "sanctification by the Spirit" (2 Thessalonians 2:13). In Romans, he speaks of it as being "transformed by the renewing of your mind" (Romans 12:2). In Hebrews, he urges us to be "partakers of His holiness" (Hebrews 12:10). And Peter encourages all believers to "grow in . . . grace" (2 Peter 3:18). In his invitation, the word *grow* isn't passive, it's active, and the action—the growing—is ongoing. The passage could be translated "keep on growing in grace."

These early Christians had already made great strides in their spiritual lives, but they were to continue to grow. Like Paul, they could say, "I press toward the goal for the prize of the upward call of God in Christ Jesus" (Philippians 3:14). The Christian life is a dynamic adventure of growth in which we ever seek to reflect the loveliness of Jesus' character more fully. We grow in grace when we experience the wonder of grace in our own lives every day. Christians long to "grow up in all things into Him who is the head—Christ" (Ephesians 4:15).

As we grow in grace, our love for God grows stronger, and our appreciation for His sacrifice on the cross deepens. The more we know Him, the more we love Him; and the more we love Him, the more our lives are changed. This is the pathway to true revival and reformation.

Reformation is simply choosing to allow the Holy Spirit to align our lives with biblical values. It is the choice to submit to God's will in every area of our lives. It is the commitment to please God in everything we do. It is the willingness to make any change necessary to live in harmony with God's commands.

Ellen White defines revival and reformation very directly: "Revival and reformation are two different things. Revival signifies a renewal of spiritual life, a quickening of the powers of mind and heart, a resurrection from spiritual death. Reformation signifies a reorganization, a change in ideas and theories, habits and practices. Reformation will not bring forth the good fruit of righteousness unless it is connected with the revival of the Spirit. Revival and reformation are to do their appointed work, and in doing this work they must blend."[1]

In those areas of our lives where, for whatever reason, we have allowed ourselves to drift from God's revealed will, revival reawakens our longings to please Him, and reformation follows as we respond to those newborn longings by surrendering anything that stands between us and Him.

When our hearts are revived, the Holy Spirit leads us to ask some heart-searching questions. Are there areas in my life that are not in harmony with God's will? Do I harbor bitterness, anger, resentment, or any other negative thoughts toward some other person? Has amusement become a god? In what I eat or the way I dress, am I clinging to an idol? Is the life I'm living one of self-centered indulgence or of unselfish service?

Still His chosen people

The Old Testament tells us that God's people frequently drifted away from Him. But that didn't make God reject them. He still considered them to be His chosen people. Time after time He sent prophets to guide His people back to Him—to lead them into a revival of their spiritual lives and a corresponding reformation.

The revivals and reformations recorded in the Old Testament have some characteristics in common. For instance, they took place when the Israelites renewed their commitment to obey God's will. It was when Israel "turned . . . to his own way" and "everyone did what was right in his own eyes" that God withdrew His blessing and the nation experienced disaster and defeat (Isaiah 53:6; Judges 21:25).

When God's people faced one of their greatest military challenges, a battle with the Ammonites and Moabites, Jehoshaphat showed remarkable spiritual leadership. Throughout the crisis, he kept the eyes of all the people focused on the power of God (2 Chronicles 20:12). He recognized something that is critical to sustaining revival and reformation: without prayer, deep repentance, and total dependence on God, the battle is lost. Judah was no match for the enemies arrayed against it. That's true of us, too—the forces of evil that we face are too powerful for us to defeat on our own.

Jehoshaphat urged his people to place their confidence in God and to believe His prophets so they would prosper (verse 20). Then he led them into a time of corporate fasting, praying, trusting, and obeying

God. "With confidence Jehoshaphat could say to the Lord, 'Our eyes are upon Thee.'. . . . Unitedly they fasted and prayed; unitedly they besought the Lord to put their enemies to confusion, that the name of Jehovah might be glorified. . . .

". . . In every emergency we are to feel that the battle is His. His resources are limitless, and apparent impossibilities will make the victory all the greater."[2]

The forces of hell are too strong for us as well. The evil one is too powerful. Without divine power, lasting change is impossible. The battle with Satan and his evil hosts cannot, will not, be won without divine intervention. In October 1863, at the height of the Civil War, Abraham Lincoln made a powerful speech similar to Jehoshaphat's. In words that speak to our hearts today, he declared,

> We have been the recipients of the choicest bounties of heaven; we have been preserved these many years in peace and prosperity; we have grown in numbers, wealth, and power as no other nation has ever grown.
>
> But we have forgotten God. We have forgotten the gracious hand which preserved us in peace and multiplied and enriched and strengthened us, and we have vainly imagined, in the deceitfulness of our hearts, that all these blessings were produced by some superior wisdom and virtue of our own. Intoxicated with unbroken success, we have become too self-sufficient to feel the necessity of redeeming and preserving grace, too proud to pray to the God that made us.[3]

How would Lincoln define *revival*? He might say it is simply renouncing all self-sufficiency and depending wholly upon God. It is recognizing that we are powerless and He is all powerful. It is trusting Him to fight our battles with Satan.

What is reformation? It is accepting the counsels of God's inspired Word, and, through the power of the Holy Spirit, living those counsels day by day. It is making any change necessary so our lives conform to His will.

Revival and reformation in Corinth

In Paul's letters to the Corinthians, he expresses great concern regarding their spiritual condition. The situation was serious. Many members had drifted away from God's ideal. The church had been torn apart by interpersonal conflicts (1 Corinthians 1:10–12; 3:3). Paul could no longer claim that the church in Corinth provided a healthy spiritual environment. He called the members "carnal" (1 Corinthians 3:1) and pointed out that they were tolerating immorality (1 Corinthians 5:1).

He noted that church members were also battling one another through lawsuits in the civil courts, which brought disrepute on the cause of Christ (1 Corinthians 6:1–7). The marriage institution was being defiled (verses 15–20). The question of eating meat offered to idols was further dividing members and fueling conflict (1 Corinthians 8). The members' celebration of the Lord's Supper made evident their self-centeredness—people were rushing to the table and grabbing for themselves all the food they could get even though it meant others went hungry (1 Corinthians 11). And finally, the Corinthian believers were also abusing the genuine gift of tongues by using it for selfish exhibitionism (1 Corinthians 14).

The Corinthian church certainly was in a real mess spiritually, but Paul didn't give up on it. His first letter to the Corinthians, whom he loved, is a stirring appeal to them to seek for revival and reformation—a call to repentance and radical change. Then, in 2 Corinthians, Paul admonished his converts again in no uncertain terms, urging them that since we have God's promises, we should "cleanse ourselves from all filthiness of flesh and spirit, perfecting holiness in the fear of God" (2 Corinthians 7:1).

Evidently, the church at Corinth responded positively to the apostle's appeals. What a change they underwent! In his first letter to the Corinthians, Paul had chastised them as being carnal. In his second letter, he says he has complete confidence in their new experience with God. Apparently, the Holy Spirit had brought revival to the Corinthians.

Commenting on this revival, Ellen White said that a "faithful messenger brought [Paul] the cheering news that a wonderful change had taken place among the Corinthian believers. Many had accepted the instruction contained in Paul's letter and had repented of their sins. Their lives were no longer a reproach to Christianity, but exerted a powerful influence in favor of practical godliness."[4]

The Corinthians still faced challenges. Trials would again test them. But they had made significant advances in the Christian faith. Spiritual revival and reformation are not some panacea that solves all of our spiritual problems. They are steps in a journey of spiritual growth— steps that draw us nearer to the heart and will of God. When God's people accept His counsel, repent of their sins, enter into heartfelt confession, and commit their lives to doing His will, God pours out His Spirit, and revival and reformation follow.

Revelation's appeal

The seven churches described in Revelation 2 and 3 are representative of the Christian church from John's time till the Second Coming. An angel instructed John to " 'write the things which you have seen, and the things which are, and the things which will take place after this' " (Revelation 1:19). The vision of the seven churches records both the triumphs and the failures of God's church—its victories and its defeats.

Although the seven churches can represent the continuum of Christian faith down through the centuries, the messages of Christ to these churches all contain lessons on revival and reformation that are vital to God's people today.

Many expositors of the prophecies of Revelation—Adventists among them—have concluded that Revelation's seven churches represent seven epochs in church history, beginning with the New Testament church. This interpretation equates Ephesus with the Christian church approximately from A.D. 31 to A.D. 100.

These early Christians were zealous for their faith. They labored unceasingly for the advancement of the gospel. They were committed to the work of the Lord. They didn't shrink from duty or responsibility.

After Jesus' ascension, His disciples diligently worked at preserving the doctrinal purity of the church. They had no tolerance for heresy and were fierce defenders of the truth. Jesus commends the church at Ephesus because they were in opposition to the Nicolaitans. Evidently, that group believed that grace relaxed some aspects of God's law. This so-called liberty or freedom led to a rather loose morality and a downplaying of the necessity of obedience. But the faithful first-century Christians stood in direct opposition to this heresy.

However, despite all the laboring for and defending of the faith done by the Christians in Ephesus, Christ regretfully spoke these words of rebuke: " ' " 'Nevertheless I have this against you, that you have left your first love' " ' " (Revelation 2:4). Apparently, the Christians of the first century faced persecution with courage and perseverance, but as time went on they began to lose their first love. What they had once done out of devotion they later did from a sense of duty. Doing Jesus' work became more important than knowing Jesus. Gradually, and almost imperceptibly, their experience with their Savior slipped away. They labored hard to defend the faith, but something vital was missing in their spiritual experience—love for Jesus and love for one another. They had the outer form of religion, but they lacked real heart conversion. They were active, but not prayerful.

Jesus urged those faltering Christians to remember, to repent, and to return. When people are empty spiritually, Jesus calls them—He calls us—to remember what it was to have our hearts filled with His grace. He calls us to remember the times when we were closest to Him. He urges us to remember those times when our hearts burned within us as we prayed and studied His Word. He calls us also to repent of our spiritual carelessness; to repent of our prayerlessness, our lack of devotional Bible study, and our loss of spiritual focus. And He calls us to return to those basic Christian practices that bring spiritual strength. He encourages us to reorder our priorities and to return to what genuine Christianity is all about.

The revelator's words are reminiscent of Hosea's appeal to Israel: "Come, and let us return to the LORD; for He has torn, but He will heal us; He has stricken, but He will bind us up. After two days He will revive us; on the third day He will raise us up, that we may live in His sight" (Hosea 6:1, 2). Revival occurs when we recognize that our spiritual experience has slipped, and we repent and once again seek the Lord with all of our hearts. And reformation follows when we realign our lives with heaven's values.

Ellen White describes the wonder of grace and the assurance of salvation this way: "Jesus loves to have us come to Him just as we are, sinful, helpless, and dependent. We may come with all our weakness, our folly, our sinfulness, and fall at His feet in penitence. It is His glory to encircle us in the arms of His love and to bind up our wounds, to cleanse us from all impurity."[5]

Understanding grace is life-transforming. It is the very essence of Christianity. God's unmerited, undeserved grace is the cornerstone of the Christian faith. Through the life, death, resurrection, and priestly ministry of Jesus, the gift of eternal life is ours. Receiving it by faith, we have the assurance of salvation.

Heaven's appeal

Seventh-day Adventism is a reform movement. God created this movement, this church, to restore biblical truths obscured in the spiritual darkness of the Middle Ages. Although the Holy Spirit worked powerfully through the Reformers, they didn't understand all the vital truths about God. There were more timeless truths He wanted His people to know. Each of these truths reveals something about God's character. God doesn't teach us things merely to fill our minds with religious knowledge. Biblical truths are windows into His heart; they reveal something about Him. The more clearly we understand the truths of His Word, the more fully we understand the depth of His love. False doctrine distorts His character. Truth unmasks the devil's lies and reveals who God really is.

From the inception of the great controversy in heaven millennia ago, Satan has attempted to malign the character of God. He has lied about God's intentions toward His creatures, but in the life Jesus lived and the truths He taught, He revealed what His heavenly Father is really like. That's why He came and lived among us.

Revelation predicts that God will raise up an end-time people to proclaim "to every nation, tribe, tongue, and people" Scripture's "everlasting gospel" of a Divine Father who loves us (Revelation 14:6). This end-time message that is to be proclaimed to the ends of the earth includes a call to loving obedience to God's will in the light of a final judgment—a judgment that will reveal to the whole universe both the justice and the mercy of God. This judgment will answer the question of fairness and will clearly reveal that in the momentous conflict between good and evil, God has always acted in the best interest of every person.

In an age in which people consider evolution to be the best answer to questions about the source and meaning of life, Jesus calls His people to worship the Creator on the Bible Sabbath. This Sabbath, the seventh-day Sabbath, speaks of life's origin, its purpose, and its destiny. It upholds Jesus, who created us, redeemed us, and is coming again for us.

The message of Revelation 14 is an urgent appeal that we return to the faith of Jesus and to keeping His commandments as we prepare for His soon return. It is a message of revival, reform, and restoration. God is appealing to His people today to be totally, unreservedly committed to Him. In Him and through Him and by Him, we can be overcomers and demonstrate to a waiting world and a watching universe the majesty of His love, the glory of His grace, and the beauty of His truth.

---

1. Ellen G. White, *Review and Herald,* February 25, 1902.

2. White, *Conflict and Courage* (Washington, D.C.: Review and Herald®, 1970), 17.

3. Abraham Lincoln, "Proclamation Appointing a National Fast Day," March 30, 1863.

4. White, *The Acts of the Apostles,* 324.

5. White, *Steps to Christ,* 52.

CHAPTER 10

Reformation: The Willingness to Grow and Change

Before Pentecost, the disciples had significant spiritual needs. Their understanding of God's plan was faulty, and they failed to comprehend Jesus' mission. But except for Judas, the disciples indeed were transformed by His marvelous grace. Christ's love broke their hearts. They experienced revival and reformation in their own lives.

A revival is simply a reawakening of deep spiritual longings. It is an intensifying of our spiritual desires as our hearts are drawn closer to God through the promptings of the Holy Spirit. Revival doesn't imply that we had no relationship with Jesus before; it just means we've answered His call to go deeper—to take another step toward Jesus. And reformation appeals to us to move beyond the status quo in our spiritual experience. It invites us to reexamine our lives in the light of biblical values and to allow the Holy Spirit to empower us to make any changes necessary for us to live in obedience to God's will.

That may be the reason reformation makes some people nervous. They are content with the status quo and don't want to change. They're afraid that the Holy Spirit might call them to surrender some relationship, some unsanctified ambition, or some other cherished idol. They have enough religion to make them comfortable, but they certainly aren't radical disciples of Jesus. Consequently, they journey through life never experiencing the joy He offers or His life-changing power. They are content to look for pennies when they could be diving for pearls. They are satisfied with the crumbs of religion when Jesus offers a banquet of heavenly delights.

When Jesus called His disciples, their attitudes and actions certainly didn't reflect the loveliness of His character, but all of that changed in the three and a half years the disciples were with Him. As they contemplated His life, their lives were changed. As they talked with Him, their talk changed. Seeing His faith, their faith grew. Sensing His commitment to His mission, they became focused on mission. Understanding the purpose for which He lived, they became purposeful too. Living with Him day by day, they became more like Him day by day.

James and John had some serious character flaws, so they weren't prepared to represent Christ's love to the world. They weren't qualified to proclaim a message of grace to others when they hadn't allowed grace to change their own lives.

> John did not naturally possess the loveliness of character that his later experience revealed. By nature he had serious defects. He was not only proud, self-assertive, and ambitious for honor, but impetuous, and resentful under injury. He and his brother were called "sons of thunder." Evil temper, the desire for revenge, the spirit of criticism, were all in the beloved disciple. But beneath all this the divine Teacher discerned the ardent, sincere, loving heart. Jesus rebuked this self-seeking, disappointed his ambitions, tested his faith. But He revealed to him that for which his soul longed—the beauty of holiness, the transforming power of love.[1]

In spite of their serious defects of character, James and John longed to reveal Jesus' character more fully. They longed for transformation of their attitudes. "The lessons of Christ, setting forth meekness and humility and love as essential to growth in grace and a fitness for His work, were of the highest value to John. He treasured every lesson and constantly sought to bring his life into harmony with the divine pattern. John had begun to discern the glory of Christ—not the worldly pomp and power for which he had been taught to hope, but 'the glory as of the Only Begotten of the Father, full of grace and truth.' John 1:14."[2]

Both John and James were willing to face their faults candidly. When the Holy Spirit pointed out defects in their characters, they repented and opened their hearts to growth. As they saw themselves as they truly were, filled with self-importance and egotistical pride, they opened their hearts to the transforming power of Jesus. And so they experienced dramatic spiritual growth. This is true reformation. Think of how the Holy Spirit empowered and used James and John in Jesus' service. While James gave his life early in his ministry, John had the joy of witnessing tens of thousands become active disciples of Christ. He saw new churches planted, new communities entered, and new countries conquered for his Lord.

The power to choose

Change comes at the point of choice. Reformation occurs as we choose to yield to the convicting power of the Holy Spirit and surrender our will to God's will. God will never force or manipulate our will. He respects our freedom. His Spirit impresses our minds, convicts our hearts, and prompts us to do the right things, but we must choose whether or not we will respond to His appeals. When we choose to change, God empowers us. Change doesn't come because we're suddenly trying harder. Reformation of character won't come because we diligently work at it. Character transformation occurs when we unite our weak, wavering will to God's almighty, unchangeable power.

A pastor friend of mine once told me about his father's battle with chewing tobacco. Wanting to be a good steward of the life God had given him, he longed to have the victory over that health-threatening addiction. But it was a real struggle. My friend remembers seeing his father begin to chew in the morning and then come to his senses and throw the wad of tobacco as far as he could out into the cornfield and declare, "I am done!" But by noon, he'd be walking up and down the rows of corn, looking for the tobacco. Do you think God would hide it from him? No, God respects our freedom of choice.

Have you ever said, "I'm finished. That's it. I won't do that again," and then a few hours later found yourself doing the thing you vowed not to do? The issue is not God's power to reform our lives and give us victory. The issue is our choices. When we want victory over some besetting sin as much as God wants us to have it, we will have it. The apostle James gives us two principles vital to overcoming: "Therefore submit to God. Resist the devil and he will flee from you. Draw near to God and He will draw near to you. Cleanse your hands, you sinners; and purify your hearts, you double-minded" (James 4:7, 8).

James's emphasis is clear. Reformation of any habit, thought, or desire comes as we do two things: submit and resist. We can't resist until we submit, but if we submit without the determination to resist in His strength, we will fail miserably. God's last-day messenger put it this way: "From first to last man is to be a laborer together with God. Unless the Holy Spirit works upon the human heart, at every step we shall stumble and fall. Man's efforts alone are nothing but worthlessness; but cooperation with Christ means a victory."[3] The changes that amount to reformation occur as we cooperate with God.

James urges us to "draw near to God" and then "cleanse your hands" and "purify your hearts." We can never do the latter until we have done the former. Drawing near to God provides the supernatural power to achieve change. Unless God empowers our choices, our best efforts will result in feeble failures.

The expression "cleanse your hands" refers to our actions—the things we do. The expression "purify your hearts" refers to our thoughts—the things we think. Reformation not only changes our actions, it also transforms our thoughts. As we cooperate with God by surrendering to His will and yielding to the promptings of the Holy Spirit, we give Him permission to work the necessary changes in our lives.

Salvation by grace really works

Salvation is only and always through grace (see Ephesians 2:8). Jesus is our Righteousness and our Redemption. He is our Savior and our

Deliverer. He is our dying Lamb, our resurrected Lord, our interceding Priest, and our coming King. He initiated the plan of salvation in eternity past, consummated the plan of salvation on the cross, is applying the plan of salvation in heaven's sanctuary, and will complete the plan of salvation at His return. Jesus convicts us of sin, draws us to Himself, places the desire to respond to His grace in our hearts, saves us, and sustains us by His grace.

However, although we are entirely dependent upon Him for our salvation, this doesn't mean we don't have a role to play in receiving His grace and being transformed by it. As the apostle Paul so forcibly stated it: "Work out your own salvation" (Philippians 2:12). In the original, the Greek word here means "carry to completion" or "carry to a full conclusion." In other words, Paul is saying, "Don't stop halfway into the Christian life. Let Jesus finish what He started in you." As *The Seventh-day Adventist Bible Commentary* so aptly puts it, "The Scriptures teach that each individual must cooperate with the will and power of God. One must 'strive to enter in' (Luke 13:24), 'put off the old man' (Col. 3:9), 'lay aside every weight,' 'run with patience' (Heb. 12:1), 'resist the devil' (James 4:7), and 'endure unto the end' (Matt. 24:13). Salvation is not of works, but it must be worked out. It springs from the mediation of Christ alone, but it is lived out by personal cooperation."[4]

We cannot work out what God hasn't worked into us. But as He works in us through His supernatural power, we are able to make the choices to "work out" in our lives the grace and strength He has worked into our lives.

As finite, sinful man works out his own salvation with fear and trembling, it is God who works in him, to will and to do of his own good pleasure. But God will not work without the cooperation of man. He must exercise his powers to the very utmost; he must place himself as an apt, willing student in the school of Christ; and as he accepts the grace that is freely offered to him, the presence of Christ in the thought and in the heart will give him decision of purpose to lay aside every weight of sin, that the heart may be filled with all the fullness of God, and of his love.[5]

Paul's admonition doesn't end with the words "work out your own salvation." He continues with this vital truth: "for it is God who works in you both to will and to do for His good pleasure" (Philippians 2:13). The Greek word behind the English translation "do" is *energein.* Our word *energy* is derived from this Greek word. William Barclay, in his Daily Study Bible series, makes this insightful comment about this unique word: "There are two significant things about that verb: it is always used of the action of God; and it is always used of effective action. The whole process of salvation is the action of God; and it is action which is effective because it is the action of God. God's action cannot be frustrated, nor can it remain half finished; it must be fully effective."[6] As we cooperate with God and allow Him to complete His work in us, He will make amazing changes in our lives. Day by day we will become more like Him. That is what reformation is all about.

Reformation occurs as we cooperate with God by choosing to surrender to Him anything in us that the Holy Spirit points out is not in harmony with His will. Unless we make those sometimes painful choices, positive, spiritual change will not occur. God won't rip selfish thoughts out of our minds despite our wishes. He won't mysteriously snatch unhealthful habits or secret indulgences out of our lives. He convicts us of sin. He convinces us of right. But He leaves the choice up to us. We must do the choosing. And when we do, He will empower us to carry out our choices.

Confidence and doubt

The experience of the disciples graphically illustrates how the Holy Spirit takes people as they are and leads them to where Jesus wants them to be. Let's consider Peter. His problem was self-confidence. He believed he was capable of facing the cross on his own. Before Peter was ready to proclaim the message of a crucified and risen Savior, his thinking had to be changed, reformed. He wasn't any match for the wiles of the evil one.

Earlier, Jesus had warned Peter, " 'Simon, Simon! Indeed, Satan has asked for you, that he may sift you as wheat. But I have prayed for you, that your faith should not fail; and when you have returned to Me, strengthen your brethren' " (Luke 22:31, 32). Jesus' statement provides a fascinating analysis of Peter's spiritual condition. Trusting in his own strength, Peter drifted from his Lord. This is why Jesus used the expression "when you have returned to Me." Peter needed a spiritual awakening. He needed a change of attitude. He needed reformation.

Think of how Peter must have felt when he heard Jesus' words, "I have prayed for you." Peter had seen the results of Jesus' prayers. He had witnessed the feeding of the five thousand, the calming of the storm on the Sea of Galilee, the deliverance of the demoniacs, and the resurrection of Lazarus. What hope Peter must have gained from knowing that Jesus was praying for him!

You are on Jesus' heart. Your name is upon His lips. He is in heaven's sanctuary praying for you. And Jesus' prayers make all the difference. He was Peter's Defender, and He is ours too—and that makes all the difference!

After Pentecost, Peter was a different man. He no longer trembled in fear at the accusations of the officers of the temple. When those religious leaders confronted him and demanded that he stop preaching in Jesus' name, he responded, " 'We ought to obey God rather than men' " (Acts 5:29).

Faith that leads to submission to Jesus' will is the most important thing in the life of every Christian. "The submission which Christ demands, the self-surrender of the will which admits truth in its sanctifying power, which trembles at the word of the Lord, are brought about by the work of the Holy Spirit. There must be a transformation of the entire being, heart, soul, and character. . . . Only at the altar of sacrifice, and from the hand of God, can the selfish, grasping man receive the celestial torch which reveals his own incompetence and leads him to submit to Christ's yoke, to learn His meekness and lowliness."[7]

Pentecost made a difference. That day a transformed Peter preached fearlessly, and three thousand were baptized (Acts 2:41). Peter realized he certainly had no strength to heal a lame man, but he also knew that

Jesus did have the necessary strength, and a miracle took place (Acts 3:9). And when the Jewish authorities attempted to silence Peter, he proclaimed, " 'We cannot but speak the things which we have seen and heard' " (Acts 4:20).

The goal of all revival is to lead us to trust Jesus rather than ourselves. It anchors us in His love and in His Word.

The conviction to return

Jesus' parable of the prodigal son has encouraged wayward children to return to their home and heartbroken parents to accept them when they come.

Jesus gets into the heart of the story this way: " 'The younger of them [two brothers] said to his father, "Father, give me the portion of the goods that falls to me." So he divided to them his livelihood' " (Luke 15:12). Selfishness motivated the young man's request. He wanted pleasure, and he wanted it now. When his father gave him his share of the inheritance, he left for a "far country." But his euphoria was short lived. When his money was gone, his "friends" were too, and he soon longed for home.

Simply put, the young man missed home too much to stay away. His heart ached to return. It is this heartache for the presence of God that leads us to long for revival and reformation in our lives. It is this heart cry for the warm embrace of the Father that leads us to make necessary changes in our lives too. But the greatest motivation we can have is the desire to stop breaking the heart of the One who loves us so much. When the prodigal son was wallowing around in the mud with the pigs, his father hurt more than he did.

When Jesus hung upon the cross, the overwhelming guilt of sin and the crushing weight of this world's condemnation broke His heart. When we grasp even faintly the pain that pierced His heart because of our sin, we will want to be done with it forever. This is especially true if we understand that sin not only brought Him pain then, but it brings Him pain now too. "Few give thought to the suffering that sin has caused our Creator. All heaven suffered in Christ's agony; but that suffering did not begin or end with His manifestation in humanity. The cross is a revelation to our dull senses of the pain that, from its very inception, sin has brought to the heart of God. Every departure from the right, every deed of cruelty, every failure of humanity to reach His ideal, brings grief to Him."[8]

The greatest motivation for change is not the pain of hell nor the delights of heaven; it is the recognition that sin brings sorrow to the One who loves us so much. Reformation occurs when my love for Him is greater than my love for anything that is not in harmony with His will. It comes when we no longer would knowingly and willing do anything that would bring pain to His heart.

Why not right now take a minute to pray, "Oh! God please give me the desire to know You in all of Your fullness, the willingness to change what You want me to change whatever the cost, and the courage to do what is right for right's sake."

---

1. Ellen G. White, *The Acts of the Apostles,* 540.

2. Ibid., 544.

3. White, *Selected Messages,* bk. 1, 381.

4. White, *The Seventh-day Adventist Bible Commentary,* 7:158.

5. White, *Fundamentals of Christian Education* (Nashville, Tenn.: Southern Publishing Association, 1923), 111.

6. William Barclay, *Letters to Philippians, Colossians, and Thessalonians,* Daily Study Bible (Philadelphia: Westminster Press, 1959), 51.

7. White, *In Heavenly Places,* 236.

8. White, *Education,* 263.

CHAPTER 11

Reformation: Thinking New Thoughts

Isaac Watts was rightly called the father of English hymnody. He is credited with writing more than 750 hymns, many of which are still sung today.

A parade was held in London to honor Watts. People thronged the streets to get a glimpse of this famous man whose songs they had sung for decades. As his carriage passed under a balcony, a woman who was astonished that the stooped, elderly man she saw on the street below was the man who had written such mighty hymns, shrieked, "What! You are Isaac Watts?"

Watts motioned for the carriage to stop and exclaimed, "Madam, could I in fancy grasp the poles or hold creation in my span, I would still be measured by my mind, for the mind is the measure of a man."

Watts was right—the mind is the measure of a man—and of a woman too. Reformation is ultimately about a changed mind, not merely changed behavior. It is about a change in our thinking—"for as [a person] thinks in his heart, so is he" (Proverbs 23:7). A reformation in our thinking will produce a reformation in our actions. Reformation occurs as the Holy Spirit brings our thoughts into harmony with Christ's thoughts. If the thoughts are right, the actions will eventually be right too.

Ellen White has informed us that "it is a law both of the intellectual and the spiritual nature, that by beholding, we become changed. The mind gradually adapts itself to the subjects upon which it is allowed to dwell. It becomes assimilated to that which it is accustomed to love and reverence. Man will never rise higher than his standard of purity or goodness or truth."[1] Change comes not as we wish for it, hope for it, or dream about it. It comes as we behold Jesus in His Word. There is nothing as spiritually transformational as prayerfully meditating on the life of Jesus and allowing the Holy Spirit to change us.

In Hebrews 2, the apostle Paul points out that although evil still reigns in this world, believers are looking somewhere else, for "we see Jesus" (Hebrews 2:9). Paul encourages us to "consider the Apostle and High Priest of our confession, Christ Jesus" (Hebrews 3:1). He says, "Seeing then that we have a great High Priest who has passed through the heavens, Jesus the Son of God, let us hold fast our confession" (Hebrews 4:14). He reveals that it is because we are "looking unto Jesus, the author and finisher of our faith" (Hebrews 12:2), that we can endure until the end. Although we may face trials and tribulation, we will triumph in Christ because "we do not look at the things which are seen, but at the things which are not seen" (2 Corinthians 4:18).

Reformation is all about looking to Jesus. It is about Jesus filling our minds. It is about Jesus shaping our thoughts. It is about Jesus guiding our actions. When we behold Jesus, He will lead us to a better way of living than the mere rigid conformity to rules produces. Focusing on Jesus rather than on rules doesn't make us any less conscientious about doing His will. Instead, it leads us to be more conscientious. We can't behold Jesus and remain the same. When we think His thoughts, we have only one desire—to please Him in everything we do.

The mind's filters

Some parents are so concerned about their children's use of the Internet that they have activated filters to block out certain sites. Others have done something similar to control what their children watch on the television. The purpose of these electronic filters is to let some things through while keeping others out. God has provided a spiritual filter for our minds. He has carefully crafted it to open our minds to only those things that will build our spiritual experience with Jesus.

The point is that we can't develop deeply spiritual thoughts if we feed our minds on violence, immorality, greed, and materialism. Our senses are the gateway to our minds. If we bombard our minds with Hollywood's stimulating entertainment, we will be molded by these sensual experiences rather than by the principles of God's Word. Those in the entertainment industry spend multiplied millions of dollars to manipulate our emotions. What they produce conditions our thinking and shapes our values. We can be assured that these entertainment gurus aren't asking, "What can we do to produce blockbuster hits that will prepare people for Jesus' return?" No, what motivates them is box office sales, with the ratings and profit they produce.

Research has repeatedly revealed the impact of media on the mind. Paul Boxer, of Rutgers University in Newark, New Jersey, was the lead researcher on a team that investigated the impact that the violence in the media has on adolescents. Boxer commented, "Even in conjunction with other factors, our research shows that media violence does enhance violent behavior. . . . On average, adolescents who were not exposed to violent media are not as prone to violent behavior." The investigators found that heavy doses of media violence were related to a higher risk of violent behavior and general aggression in adolescents. Even teens at low risk of violence overall seem to be vulnerable to the influence of media violence. Based on these and other findings, Boxer and his colleagues conclude that "there currently can be very little doubt that exposure to violence in the media has a consistent and substantial impact on aggressive behavior."[2]

Another study looked at teens in both Japan (which is considered to be a low-violence culture) and the United States (considered to be a high-violence culture). The researchers there found that teens who frequently play violent video games behave more aggressively than their classmates who don't play those games. And the February 2009 *American Journal of Nursing* reported the findings of a study of the relationship between television-viewing habits and teenage pregnancy. "A total of 2,003 teens (ages 12 to 17 years) were asked how often they watched

23 popular TV shows that portrayed passionate kissing, sexual talk, and sexual intercourse. One to three years later they were interviewed again; 744 teens reported being sexually active. Those who watched the most TV shows with sexual content were two to three times more likely to become pregnant or to impregnate someone than were teens who watched the least."

An admonition given by the apostle Paul echoes down the centuries: "Whatever things are true, whatever things are noble, whatever things are just, whatever things are pure, whatever things are lovely, whatever things are of good report, if there is any virtue and if there is anything praiseworthy—meditate on these things" (Philippians 4:8). Seventh-day Adventist Christians preparing for the second coming of Christ ought to avoid sacrificing their souls on the altar of this world's entertainment. If the devil dominates your thoughts by replaying TV, movie, and other media images again and again in your mind, you will become drunk with the intoxicating pleasures of this world and numb to eternal values. Through the prophetic gift, God has given Seventh-day Adventists unique insight into preparation for the coming of the Lord. Ellen White exposed the delusions of Satan in this insightful statement:

It is the special work of Satan in these last days to take possession of the minds of youth, to corrupt the thoughts, and inflame the passions; for he knows that by so doing he can lead to impure actions, and thus all the noble faculties of the mind will become debased, and he can control them to suit his own purposes. All are free moral agents, and as such they must train their thoughts to run in the right channel. The first work of those who would reform is to purify the imagination. Our meditations should be such as will elevate the mind.[3]

God calls us to avoid being squeezed into the mold of this world. He calls us instead to be transformed into the image of Christ by the renewing of our minds. The Greek word translated as "transformed" is *metamorphoō*, from which we get the word *metamorphosis*. This word is used of caterpillars, which crawl around until they are changed—

transformed into butterflies—and live a new and entirely different life. Through the power of the Holy Spirit, believers are metamorphosed, too, and they live an entirely different life than they did when under the power of sin (2 Corinthians 3:18).

Jesus compared this change to a new birth. It means taking on a new way of thinking—which always leads to a new way of living. Paul called it "the washing of regeneration and renewing of the Holy Spirit" (Titus 3:5). He spoke of the inward person—our thinking patterns—being renewed day by day (2 Corinthians 4:16). These passages don't mean that we must spend every waking moment contemplating spiritual things. They don't advocate a monastic lifestyle of continual prayer and meditation. But these verses do mean that our relationship with Jesus must govern every aspect of our lives. They do advocate a mindset that makes eternal values the foundation for all that we think, say, and do. When Jesus is the center of our lives, everything else becomes subject to Him.

The main entrance to a great cathedral in Milan, Italy, has three large doors. Inscribed above the left-hand door are the words, "All that pleases is but for a moment," and over the right-hand door, "All that troubles is but for a moment." Emblazoned in bold letters over the center door is this important reminder: "That alone endures which is eternal." The most important choices we can ever make are those that have eternal consequences. May we choose wisely!

The mind's safeguard

The apostle Paul admonishes us to "let this mind be in you which was also in Christ Jesus" (Philippians 2:5). The word *let* means "to allow or to permit." *The Pulpit Commentary* contains an interesting observation regarding this passage. The translation of the passage made by the author of the commentary on Philippians reads, "Mind the things the Lord Jesus minded." Then he wrote that Paul encourages us to love what Jesus loved and hate what He hated, and he added this thought: "The thoughts, desires, motives of the Christian should be the thoughts, desires, motives which filled the sacred heart of Jesus Christ our Lord. We must strive to imitate Him, to reproduce His image, not only in the outward, but even in the inner life."[4] Fixing our minds on heavenly things produces heavenly thoughts. Fixing our minds on earthly things produces earthly thoughts. It's that simple.

The apostle also writes about "bringing every thought into captivity to the obedience of Christ" (2 Corinthians 10:4). What did he mean? Perhaps the old saying, "You can't stop the birds from flying over your head, but you can stop them from nesting in your hair," says it best. Sights, sounds, and smells raise thoughts in our minds. We can't control what thoughts pop up—but we *can* choose which thoughts we'll dwell upon and allow to dominate our thinking. We can't banish all carnal thoughts by merely wishing they would go away, but we can push them out by filling our minds with other, better thoughts. A mind that is focused on the positive principles of God's Word is a mind that God's grace protects from the wiles of the evil one.

Bible writers use a variety of terms to describe Christian growth. They speak of "[growth] in the grace," "being sanctified," going "on to perfection," "completeness" (AMP), living in "the Spirit of God," and being "partakers of His holiness" (2 Peter 3:18; Hebrews 2:11; 6:1; Romans 8:9; and Hebrews 12:10). This growth includes every aspect of our lives.

The ancient Greeks were dualistic; they believed one could separate the soul from the body. But the disciples taught that physical, mental, emotional, and spiritual health were interconnected and couldn't be separated. Whatever affects one part of a person affects all parts of that person. The Bible indicates that preparation for our Lord's return involves every aspect of our lives. Paul concludes his first letter to the Thessalonians with a prayer for them: "Now may the God of peace Himself sanctify you completely" (1 Thessalonians 5:23). The Greek word translated as "completely" is *holoteleis,* which conveys the idea of being complete in all parts. We can't withhold any part of our lives from Jesus. He longs to transform us entirely—our thinking, our habits, and the things we do that make up our lifestyles. Sin retained in any part of our lives undermines our faith.

Scripture indicates that our physical, mental, and emotional well-being are indissolubly linked to our spiritual well-being. The apostle

Paul appealed to believers to glorify God in their bodies. He believed that we are not our own and all humanity was "bought at a price" (1 Corinthians 6:19, 20). Caring for our bodies by adopting a healthful lifestyle means much more than merely adding a few more years to our lives. It is an act of worship to the Christ who created us and redeemed us.

The Holy Spirit doesn't limit Himself to one aspect of our lives when He convicts us of our need for growth. Reformation is not one dimensional. The Spirit longs to bring every part of our lives into total conformity to the will of Christ. If there are physical lifestyle practices not in harmony with God's will, He invites us to surrender them for His glory.

Satan wants to control our minds through our bodies. Jesus longs to control our bodies through our minds. Ellen White tells us, "Health is an inestimable blessing and one more closely related to conscience and religion than many realize. It has a great deal to do with one's capability for service and should be as sacredly guarded as the character, for the more perfect the health the more perfect will be our efforts for the advancement of God's cause and for the blessing of humanity."[5]

One of the great reforms God is calling for is health reform—not as a means of self-righteousness, but as a means of preparing people for the coming of Jesus. Our bodies are temples, not funhouses. Are there some areas of your physical life you have not fully surrendered to Christ? Are there articles of diet you have not surrendered? Does your exercise consist of changing the channels on the television via the remote as you lie on the couch? Are you overworking and underexercising, pushing yourself with very little sleep? By following heaven's principles, we can live more joy-filled, productive, abundant, healthy lives and be more powerful witnesses to the world. Jesus said, " 'I have come that they may have life, and that they may have it more abundantly' " (John 10:10).

Images of influence

Jesus used many metaphors to describe Himself and His church. One that He used frequently is light. He is " 'the light of the world' "

(John 8:12); the "true Light which gives light to every man coming into the world" (John 1:9). He encourages us to walk in the light and to " 'believe in the light' " (John 12:35, 36).

The goal of all reformation is to allow the light of Jesus' love, grace, and truth to shine through us to light the lives of others. Light shines in contrast to the darkness. Jesus has called His people to a lifestyle distinctly different from that of the world to demonstrate the superiority of His way of life. He calls us to be compassionate, caring, and concerned in a world of selfishness, greed, and egotism (Matthew 20:28). He calls us to high standards in entertainment in a society intoxicated with pleasure (Colossians 3:1, 2). He calls us to healthful living at a time when millions are dying too young from self-inflicted degenerative diseases (John 10:10). In the midst of an immodest, sex-centered, thrill-jaded generation, Jesus calls us to modesty, propriety, and moral purity (1 Peter 3:3, 4).

God's ideal for His church and for us as individuals is higher than we can imagine. He longs to reveal His character of love through His people. Reformation means allowing the Holy Spirit to work through us so that we live in harmony with our high calling in Christ. It includes a transformation in our thought patterns that leads to a transformation in what we do. A reformed life is one in which maintaining the status quo is no longer acceptable. It is one in which being a Christian in name only is replaced with a heart burning passionately for Christ. It is one in which formalism and a focus on externals fades into insignificance in the light of a vibrant, living experience with Jesus Christ.

William Dunn Longstaff was a Christian businessman who lived in England in the latter part of the nineteenth century. One day as Longstaff sat in church listening to a missionary from China preach on 1 Peter 1:16, " 'Be holy, for I am holy,' " something stirred deep within his soul. He sensed that God was leading him to a richer, fuller experience. In response, he wrote what has become a familiar hymn.

Read the first two verses of this old hymn as a prayer, letting God speak to your heart.

Take time to be holy, speak oft with thy Lord;
  Abide in Him always, and feed on His Word.
Make friends of God's children, help those who are weak,
  Forgetting in nothing His blessing to seek.

Take time to be holy, the world rushes on;
  Spend much time in secret with Jesus alone;
By looking to Jesus, like Him thou shalt be;
  Thy friends in thy conduct His likeness shall see.

---

1. Ellen G. White, *The Great Controversy*, 555.

2. Tudor Vieru, "Violence in the Media Makes Children More Aggressive," *Softpedia*, November 27, 2008, accessed March 27, 2013, http://news.softpedia.com/news/Violence-in-the-Media-Makes-Children-More-Aggressive-98749.shtml.

3. White, *Christian Temperance and Bible Hygiene* (Grand Rapids, Mich.: Good Health Publishing Company, 1890), 136.

4. H. D. M. Spence and Joseph S. Exell, eds., *The Epistle to the Philippians, The Pulpit Commentary* (Grand Rapids, Mich.: William B. Eerdman's Publishing Company, 1962), 20:59.

5. Ellen G. White, *Counsels to Parents, Teachers, and Students* (Mountain View, Calif.: Pacific Press®, 1943), 294.

CHAPTER 12

Reformation: Healing Broken Relationships

Reformation requires restored relationships. Fractured relationships hinder the outpouring of the Holy Spirit in His fullness. Unless broken relationships are mended, the latter rain—heaven's end-time blessing meant to finish God's mission on earth—will not come. In the first century, the upper-room experience united believers in a bond of fellowship that prepared them to receive the Holy Spirit's fullness at Pentecost. When the church is not united, its witness to the world is muted.

Even after Pentecost, there were times when the relationships between believers were strained. The New Testament records repeated examples of church leaders and individual members dealing with these challenging circumstances. There are, for example, the stories of the conflicts that arose between Paul, on one hand, and Barnabas and John Mark on the other; between Philemon and Onesimus; and in the church at Corinth. And, of course, standing head and shoulders above them all is the conflict between Jesus and those who crucified Him—a conflict that reveals the depths of divine forgiveness. The principles we find in these stories are extremely valuable for the church today—revealing, as they do, how to deal with conflict and the positive results obtained when people follow these principles.

The great spiritual revivals of the past fostered the healing of relationships. The work of the Holy Spirit drew people closer to God and to one another. The greatest demonstration of the truthfulness of the gospel is not necessarily what the church says, but how church members live. Jesus Himself said, " 'By this all will know that you are My disciples, if you have love for one another' " (John 13: 35).

Paul was passionate about sharing Jesus. He was a man on a mission. Barnabas joined his evangelistic endeavors, and the two of them formed a fearless evangelistic team. Their relationship functioned on several levels: they were friends, working associates, and fellow Christians. But eventually a conflict arose between them—one that involved John Mark. Evidently, this young preacher left his post in Pamphylia when things became difficult there. Ellen White tells us: "This desertion caused Paul to judge Mark unfavorably, and even severely, for a time. Barnabas, on the other hand, was inclined to excuse him because of his inexperience. He felt anxious that Mark should not abandon the ministry, for he saw in him qualifications that would fit him to be a useful worker for Christ."[1]

Although Paul and Barnabas had a deep respect for one another, the conflict over John Mark led them to separate from one another. Paul invited Silas to accompany him on his preaching tours, and Barnabas and John Mark formed an evangelistic team of their own.

God used both of these evangelistic teams to plant new churches and win new converts, yet there were still issues between them that they needed to resolve. God's ultimate goal for Paul, Barnabas, and John Mark was reconciliation. He longed for their relationship to be restored. The apostle who preached grace needed to extend grace to the young preacher who had deserted him. The apostle of forgiveness needed to forgive the young man who had wronged him. The persecutor of Christians who had been given a second chance needed to offer the young man who had lost his nerve a second chance.

Although some of the details of Paul's reconciliation with John Mark may be a little sketchy, the biblical record does make it clear that the relationship was restored. Paul noticed John Mark's growth in grace, and that touched the veteran evangelist's heart. He reached out to the young man, and John Mark became one of his most trusted companions. Eventually, Paul recommended John Mark to the church at Colossae as a "fellow [worker] for the kingdom of God" (Colossians 4:10, 11). And at the end of his life, he asked Timothy to bring John Mark with him to Rome—because, he said, John Mark was "useful to me for ministry" (2 Timothy 4:11). The barrier between them was broken down. God's grace had healed a fractured relationship. And Paul's ministry was enriched by the young preacher whom he had forgiven.

Think of the joy the apostle Paul would have missed if he hadn't been willing to forgive. Think of the joy John Mark would have missed if he had wallowed in bitterness and rejected Paul's forgiveness of his cowardice. People who won't forgive can't have deep relationships, so they miss much of life's joy.

From slave to son

While Paul was imprisoned in Rome, he met a runaway slave named Onesimus. This slave had fled from Colossae to Rome, evidently hoping to start a new life there. Paul knew this slave's master, Philemon. In fact, he calls Philemon his "beloved friend and fellow laborer" (Philemon 1). The epistle of Philemon is Paul's appeal to his friend to forgive Onesimus and restore their relationship.

Philemon was a leader of the church in Colossae. If he harbored bitterness toward Onesimus, it would color his Christian witness. And if Onesimus, a recent convert, didn't make things right with his master, his experience with Jesus would be seriously affected. Relationships matter not only because they are critically important for the harmony of the church, but also for the spiritual growth of the people involved. As difficult as it may sound, we cannot know grace until we extend it to others, and we cannot experience forgiveness in all of its wonder and beauty unless we're willing to forgive.

In his epistle to the Galatians, Paul had thundered, "There is neither Jew nor Greek, there is neither slave nor free, thee is neither male nor female; for you are all one in Christ Jesus" (Galatians 3:28). So we may find it somewhat surprising that Paul didn't write to Philemon about the evils of slavery. But Paul's strategy was far more effective than direct confrontation would have been. He sent Onesimus back to Philemon not as a slave but as his own "son" in Jesus and Philemon's "beloved brother . . . in the Lord" (Philemon 16).

Runaway slaves faced a dismal future. At best, they were doomed to a life of destitution and poverty, and if caught, they faced punishment that ranged from a severe whipping to execution. But as Philemon's brother in Christ and a now-willing worker, Onesimus's food, lodging, and job were secure. So, the restoration of this broken relationship made a dramatic difference in both his life in this age and his eternal destiny. He became "a faithful and beloved brother" and a coworker with both Philemon and Paul in the cause of Christ (Colossians 4:9). A second-century account says that Ignatius, one of the leaders of the Christian church in the generation after the disciples, met Onesimus in Ephesus, where he had become one of the spiritual leaders in the local church.

Reconciliation made a difference. God had plans for this runaway slave, and the healing of his fractured relationship with Philemon pushed those plans along.

Does God have amazing plans for your life that would be advanced by the mending of some broken relationship? Could God be calling for a change—a reformation—in your relationship to an estranged family member or a former friend? Might the Holy Spirit be impressing you to take the initiative to restore that relationship? If you don't take the initiative, the relationship may never be restored. Think of the blessings that both you and that other person would then miss.

From comparison to complement

We see intention for our relationships in the church of Corinth also. That church was fraught with conflict. The members identified themselves as followers of Apollos, of Peter, or of Paul, and they built mental walls that divided the church. Their animosities had made them carnal, not spiritual, so envy and strife were common. The church's attitudes and actions certainly didn't reflect the love of Jesus. Its members didn't act like people whose hearts had been converted and whose lives had been transformed. That church needed a reformation.

In Paul's letters to the Corinthians, he outlined critical principles of church unity. He pointed out that Jesus uses different people to do different ministries in His church and that though the members' roles differed, each of them was a laborer together with God for the building up of His kingdom (1 Corinthians 3:9).

God calls us to cooperate, not to compete. Each believer is gifted by God to minister to the body of Christ and serve the community (1 Corinthians 12:11). Christ's church needs the gifts of all the believers (verses 18–23). Those gifts are not meant to show God's favor of some over others. He gives them so we can serve people in need. All comparisons with others, then, are unwise. Comparisons make us feel either discouraged or proud, and both of these attitudes cripple our effectiveness for Christ. As we labor within the sphere of influence that Christ has given us, we will find joy and contentment in our witness. Our labors will complement the efforts of other members, and the church of Christ will make giant strides toward the kingdom.

Ellen White points out, "When the laborers have an abiding Christ in their own souls, when all selfishness is dead, when there is no rivalry, no strife for the supremacy, when oneness exists, when they sanctify themselves, so that love for one another is seen and felt, then the showers of the grace of the Holy Spirit will just as surely come upon them as that God's promise will never fail in one jot or tittle."[2] Conflicts between leaders and members of the church bring disrepute on the body of Christ. But when friction is broken down and the combatants are reconciled, God's name is honored and His cause advanced.

Back in the nineteenth century, Charles Spurgeon and Joseph Parker were pastors in London. One Sunday, Parker commented from his pulpit that the children admitted to Spurgeon's orphanage came there in extremely poor condition. Unfortunately, someone told Spurgeon that Parker said Spurgeon's orphanage was in poor condition.

The next Sunday, Spurgeon blasted Parker from the pulpit. His attack was printed in the newspapers and became the talk of the town. So, the following Sunday, people flocked to Parker's church to hear him fire volleys back at Spurgeon. Instead, Parker said, "I understand Dr. Spurgeon is not in his pulpit today, and this is the Sunday they use to take an offering for the orphanage. I suggest we take a love offering here instead."

The crowd was delighted. The ushers had to empty the offering plates three times to handle all the money that people gave. Later that week Spurgeon knocked on Parker's door, and when Parker answered the knock, Spurgeon said, "You know, Parker; you have practiced grace on me. You have given me not what I deserved; you have given me what I needed."[3]

Pastor Parker's grace-filled attitude honored God and demonstrated to observers the reality of the gospel.

The apostle Paul urges us to cease making comparisons and to banish competition. Cooperation and complement, compassion and concern, are characteristics of healthy churches.

Bitterness blocks the blessings of God. Envy eats away at our enthusiasm for the things of the kingdom. Division destroys our delight in Jesus. But forgiveness opens the clogged channels of the heart. It prepares us to receive Jesus' greatest blessings.

Just what is forgiveness? Does forgiveness justify the behavior of someone who has horribly wronged us? What if the person we're keeping at a distance doesn't deserve our forgiveness? What if that person isn't repentant?

The Gospels answer these questions. Christ took the initiative in reconciling us to Himself. His forgiveness doesn't depend on our repentance. He forgives us before we repent in order to bring us to repentance. It is "the goodness of God [that] leads [us] to repentance" (Romans 2:4). In Christ, we were reconciled to God while we were yet sinners. Our repentance and confession don't create reconciliation; Christ's death on the cross did that. His death on the cross reconciled us to God while "we were [yet] enemies" (Romans 5:10). It is certainly true that we cannot receive God's grace without repenting and confessing, but our repentance doesn't create forgiveness in God's heart that was not there before. It enables us to receive it.

Forgiveness is both something we think and feel and something we do. God modeled forgiveness in the person of Jesus Christ. He doesn't forgive us because we are worthy. It is accepting the forgiveness He freely offers that makes us worthy. We aren't forgiven because we are righteous. It is when Jesus forgives us that we become righteous. In one of the most amazing passages in the Bible, Paul portrays the magnitude of God's love: "The proof of God's amazing love is this: that it was while we were sinners that Christ died for us" (verse 8, Phillips).

In our sinful natures we were hostile toward God; but He took the initiative and reconciled us to Himself through the death of His Son. Since He reached out to us when we hadn't yet reached out to Him, we ought to reach out to others even though they aren't reaching out to us. Since He forgave us when we didn't deserve it, we should forgive others when they don't deserve it.

Forgiving people doesn't justify their behavior toward us. It just means that because Christ doesn't condemn us, we don't condemn them. We can be reconciled to those who have wronged us because Christ reconciled us to Himself when we were wronging Him. We can forgive because we are forgiven. We can love because we are loved. Forgiveness is a choice. We can choose to forgive in spite of other people's actions or attitudes toward us. This is the true spirit of Jesus.

As I mentioned previously, it is true that we can't receive the blessings of forgiveness until we confess our sins. But this doesn't mean that our confession creates forgiveness in God's heart. Forgiveness was in His heart all the time. Our confession enables us to receive that forgiveness (1 John 1:9). Confession is vitally important not because it changes God's attitude toward us, but because it changes our attitude toward Him. When we yield to the Holy Spirit's convicting power and repent and confess our sin, we are changed.

Failure to forgive someone who has wronged us hurts us more than it hurts that other person—even if that person doesn't deserve our forgiveness. If you refuse to forgive, you are adding pain to the pain of the injury you already received. Shortly after World War II, Corrie ten Boom, who had suffered the horrors of a Nazi concentration camp, traveled throughout Germany preaching a message of forgiveness. Corrie made this insightful observation: the people who were able to forgive could move on with their lives. Their wounds healed. Those who didn't forgive were locked in the past and doomed by it. The decision to forgive made all the difference.

From rancor to restoration

In Matthew 18, Jesus declares, " 'If your brother sins against you, go and tell him his fault between you and him alone' " (Matthew 18:15). Jesus' intention is that we keep the conflict in as small a circle as possible. He wants the two people involved to solve the problem themselves. People often become much more defensive when they feel other people are denigrating them in a public way, but a climate of reconciliation is created when Christians work at settling their differences privately in the spirit of Christian love and mutual understanding. Then the atmosphere is right for the Holy Spirit to work with them to resolve their differences.

Ellen White gives us divine insight: "In the spirit of meekness, 'considering thyself, lest thou also be tempted,' (Gal. 6:1), go to the erring one, and 'tell him his fault between thee and him alone.' Do not put him to shame by exposing his fault to others, nor bring dishonor upon Christ by making public the sin or error of one who bears His name."[4] When we're dealing with conflict, the loving, forgiving Spirit of Jesus makes all the difference. In the spirit of Jesus, share your heart's burdens and concerns. If you have wronged your brother or sister, ask for forgiveness. Pray together, seeking to love one another.

There are times when personal appeals for conflict resolution are ineffective. In these instances, Jesus invites us to take two or possibly three others with us. They should come with an attitude of Christian love and compassion as counselors and prayer partners.

We should take this second step in the reconciliation process only after we've taken the first one. If we haven't approached the offender individually and attempted to deal with the issue, we shouldn't attempt to resolve it in a group setting. The more people who are involved in a problem, the greater the likelihood of magnified misunderstandings. People will be tempted to take sides and to become hardened in their positions. Jesus intended the process He set forth to bring people together, not to drive them further apart. He meant it to restore relationships, not to prove who is right.

Occasionally, all attempts to solve the problem fail. In that case, Jesus instructs us to bring the issue before the church. He doesn't mean that we should interrupt the Sabbath morning worship service with personal conflicts. The church board is the appropriate forum for working through the issues that the first two steps don't resolve. Again, Christ's purpose is reconciliation. It is not to place blame on one party and exonerate the other. Following Christ's instructions brings unity to His church. Love wins.

Author and teacher Dr. Howard Hendricks tells the story of a young man who strayed from the Lord but was finally brought back by the help of a friend. Hendricks asked this renewed Christian how he felt while he was away from the Lord.

The young man said it seemed like he was out at sea, in deep water—deep trouble—and all his friends were on the shore hurling accusations at him about justice, penalty, and wrong. "But," he said, "there was one Christian brother who actually swam out to get me and would not let me go. I fought him, but he pushed aside my fighting, grasped me, put a life jacket around me, and took me to shore. By the grace of God, he was the reason I was restored. He would not let me go."[5]

We, too, must not give up on people and our relationship with them too easily. May God's grace make us less judgmental and more forgiving. May we—you and I and our churches—be ambassadors of reconciliation rather than agents of condemnation.

---

1. Ellen G. White, *The Acts of the Apostles*, 170.

2. White, *Selected Messages*, bk. 1 (Washington, D.C.: Review and Herald®, 1958), 175.

3. "Spurgeon's Orphanage," *Moody Monthly*, December 1983, 81, quoted in Bible.org, accessed March 27, 2013, http://bible.org/illustration/spurgeon%E2%80%99s-orphanage.

4. White, *The Desire of Ages*, 440.

5. "Sermon Illustrations, Stories," SermonCentral, accessed March 27, 2013, http://www.sermoncentral.com/illustrations/sermon-illustration-stories-1274.asp.

CHAPTER 13

The Promised Revival: God's Mission Accomplished

The challenge of taking God's last-day message to the entire world in this generation may seem impossible. From a human perspective the obstacles are formidable. Consider the sheer numbers. True, the membership of the Seventh-day Adventist Church—baptized members and their children—is approaching 25 million. But there are more than 7 billion people on our planet, and only 2.2 billion of them call themselves Christian. The church is growing rapidly, but, unfortunately, it isn't keeping up with the growth of the world's population, and there are multiple areas where the name *Seventh-day Adventist* is still unknown.

These sobering figures make us ask some serious questions. *Can* the gospel be preached to the entire world in this generation? How will the work of God on earth be finished? Will some breakthrough dramatically speed up the proclamation of the messages borne to earth by Revelation's three angels?

These questions might disturb us—until we remember that though God has given us the privilege of cooperating with Him in His work, ultimately, the mission is His, and He will accomplish it. It is the outpouring of the Holy Spirit in latter-rain power that will finally complete God's work on earth.

The promised power

Jesus' great commission, "Go into all the world" (see Matthew 28:18–20), is accompanied by His great promise. His followers preach the gospel by His authority and in His power. He has promised His church that as they carry out the mission, He will be with them " 'always, even to the end of the age' " (verse 20). In Jesus' life, death, and resurrection, He triumphed over all the forces of evil, including all evil spirits, demonic forces, disease, and death. He is the Master of every situation.

The Gospel of Matthew shows that Jesus has authority over the forces of evil. He has already triumphed over the forces of hell, and when we step out in faith to share Jesus' message with others, we go in His authority and with His power. He supplies us with wisdom, strength, and courage. Ellen White says that when Jesus gave His disciples their commission, "He made full provision for the prosecution of the work, and took upon Himself the responsibility for its success. So long as they obeyed His word, and worked in connection with Him, they could not fail."[1]

Jose and Sonya were godly, humble Adventists who believed that the Holy Spirit would empower them to be witnesses for Jesus in spite of their limitations. They didn't appear to be the best candidates to share God's Word with others. They didn't have many of the qualities generally considered necessary to be effective witnesses. However, they did have the one quality that matters most: hearts surrendered to God and filled with the Holy Spirit.

Jose lived in a small farming community. He had grown up without the advantage of an education. Even as an adult he couldn't read or write. But his children could, so he asked them to read the Bible to him. In this way he memorized hundreds of Bible texts.

One day the Holy Spirit impressed him to share his faith with other people. So he began visiting other families in his community with his Bible in his hand. He would tell the people he met that he couldn't read and ask them to read a passage in the Bible for him. He directed those who agreed to read to him to texts on topics such as salvation, the second coming of Christ, and the Sabbath. Jose visited these people every week, and in time, many of his readers agreed to further study and eventually were baptized!

Sonya is blind, but she has real spiritual eyesight. With a friend as her guide, she walks through the streets of the city in southern India where she lives, knocking on the doors of one person after another and asking them if they would like her to pray with them. Through her prayer ministry, she has developed scores of spiritual friends, many of whom have taken Bible studies and been baptized.

The stories of Jose and Sonya tell us an eternal truth: God doesn't call the qualified; He qualifies those He calls. He uses those who are willing, empowers them, and sends them out to witness for Him. The Great Commission Jesus gave isn't for a select few. It is for all the church—for every member. When Jesus has a people totally committed to Him and willing to share His love and truth with the people around them, He will pour out His Holy Spirit in latter-rain power for the finishing of His work.

The Great Commission Jesus has given us calls for us to go to " 'all the nations' " (Matthew 28:19). The original Greek text reads *ta ethnē,* which literally means "all ethnic groups," or "all peoples." Jesus has commissioned His church to proclaim the gospel of His love and truth to every person in every village, town, city, state, province, and country in the world. The task is great, but our God is greater.

Jesus had promised His disciples that He would " 'send the promise of [His] Father,' " and they would receive power from on high (Luke 24:49). Acts makes it very explicit: " 'You shall receive power when the Holy Spirit has come upon you; and you shall be witnesses to Me in Jerusalem, and in all Judea and Samaria, and to the end of the earth' " (Acts 1:8).

No matter how apparently challenging the situation, the promises of God are sure. The proclamation of the gospel to the entire world in this generation may seem impossible, but God's power will overcome every obstacle. The powers of hell will be defeated. Before the return of our Lord, every person on planet Earth will have a reasonable opportunity to hear and understand God's message of love and truth.

The Promised Revival: God's Mission Accomplished

An all-encompassing promise

The story told in the book of Acts isn't one of a few isolated individuals here and there receiving the outpouring of the Holy Spirit. It's the story of the whole church receiving the mighty outpouring of the Spirit. The whole church prayed. The whole church confessed. The whole church repented. The whole church committed itself to mission. The whole church sought the infilling of the Holy Spirit. And God answered, and the whole church opened its heart to this blessing of God. Let's review that upper-room prayer meeting once again.

"These all continued with one accord in prayer and supplication, with the women and Mary the mother of Jesus" (Acts 1:14). The 120 believers that comprised this fledgling church earnestly sought God in prayer (verse 15). They prayed for the promised outpouring of the Holy Spirit. They recognized their inability to reach the world with the story of the Resurrected Lord. And as they prayed, confessing their sins and pleading with God for power to proclaim His grace, the floodgates of heaven opened, and the rain of the Spirit poured down upon them. Luke described the scene this way: "They were *all* filled with the Holy Spirit and began to speak with other tongues, as the Spirit gave them utterance" (Acts 2:4; emphasis added).

Notice that the text says "they *all* were filled with the Holy Spirit." Who were the "all" that were filled? The word doesn't mean just all the apostles. It means all of those who were in the upper room—all 120 believers.

Peter recognized what happened to those in the upper room to be a fulfillment of a prophecy in the Old Testament's book of Joel. When he explained what was happening, he quoted that prophecy: " ' "It shall come to pass in the last days, says God, that I will pour out of My Spirit on *all* flesh; your sons and your daughters shall prophesy, your young men shall see visions, your old men shall dream dreams. And on My menservants and on My maidservants I will pour out My Spirit in those days" ' " (Acts 2:17, 18; emphasis added).

God pays no attention to gender—the Holy Spirit was poured out without measure on males and females alike. God pays no attention to age—the Holy Spirit was poured out without measure on the young and old alike. God pays no attention to status—the Holy Spirit was poured out without measure on household servants and common laborers and rich people and Pharisees alike.

That outpouring of the Holy Spirit had a dramatic effect: three thousand were baptized in one day! God did what those first-century believers never dreamed possible. When they woke up on Pentecost morning, they were a struggling band of believers. When they went to bed that night, they were a force to be reckoned with. And here is some incredibly good news for God's people today: "These scenes are to be repeated, and with greater power. The outpouring of the Holy Spirit on the day of Pentecost was the former rain, but the latter rain will be more abundant."[2] "The lapse of time has wrought no change in Christ's parting promise to send the Holy Spirit as His representative. It is not because of any restriction on the part of God that the riches of His grace do not flow earthward to men. If the fulfillment of the promise is not seen as it might be, it is because the promise is not appreciated as it should be. If *all* were willing, *all* would be filled with the Spirit."[3]

Throughout Old Testament times, God poured out His Holy Spirit on individuals, but at Pentecost, He poured out His Holy Spirit on His entire church. And when the members of that church were filled with God's Spirit, the gospel message that they bore changed the world.

God longs to do that again. He longs to pour His Spirit upon males and females, young and old, rich and poor, the educated and the uneducated. The promise of the Spirit is all-embracing. It is for you, and it is for me. It is for your congregation and for the entire, world-wide body of Seventh-day Adventists. It is ours. We can claim it today. Jesus longs to fill us with the power of His Spirit right now.

How can we receive this infilling of the Holy Spirit individually? And how can the whole church receive this mighty outpouring?

While God has promised to give His Holy Spirit to His people in earth's last days, there are conditions to be met. God won't pour out His Spirit if we're not praying for it. Luke says the church in his day "all continued with one accord in prayer" (Acts 1:14). Ellen White notes, "We should pray as earnestly for the descent of the Holy Spirit as the disciples prayed on the day of Pentecost."[4] Zechariah has told us to "ask the Lord for rain in the time of the latter rain" (Zechariah 10:1).

Jesus gives us the following encouragement: " 'If you then, being evil, know how to give good gifts to your children, how much more will your heavenly Father give the Holy Spirit to those who ask Him!' " (Luke 11:13). And Ellen White counseled, "My brethren and sisters, plead for the Holy Spirit, God stands back of every promise He has made."[5]

Steps to spiritual revival

Back in chapter 5, I mentioned the spiritual revival that shook Wales in 1904. Someone asked Evan Roberts, the young man through whom the Holy Spirit got it started, what were the steps one must take to start such a revival. He said seek God and confess all known sin, get rid of anything that might hinder one's relationship with Jesus, obey the Spirit instantly and unreservedly, and confess Christ publicly.

Revival will come when we earnestly petition God for a fresh anointing of the Holy Spirit daily. The power of revival will fall upon us when we consecrate everything we have and are to God. We must listen to what the Holy Spirit says to us through God's Word, follow His guidance immediately, and tell others what God is doing in our lives.

We must not hesitate to speak of God's love and grace to the people God brings into our lives. The fullness of the Holy Spirit's power will be poured out only on a praying, committed, united, witnessing church. Self-centeredness, pride, and competition limit what God can do through us. His power will be unleashed when we allow Him to reign supreme in our lives. His power will be poured out when we give Him the glory for whatever He accomplishes through us. His power will come when we love the lost as He loves the lost. Holy Spirit power will fall from heaven when the things that matter the most to us are the things that matter the most to Him.

The early and the latter rains

Both the Old and New Testaments use water as a symbol of the Holy Spirit. Through the prophet Isaiah, our Lord promised, " ' "I will pour water on him who is thirsty, . . . I will pour My Spirit on your descendants" ' " (Isaiah 44:3). We find the same parallelism and symbolism in the book of Joel. God promises to water Israel's fields and then declares, " 'It shall come to pass afterward that I will pour out My Spirit on all flesh' " (Joel 2:23, 28). Jesus also used water to represent the Holy Spirit. John tells us that during the Feast of Tabernacles, Jesus went into the temple and proclaimed, " 'He who believes in Me, as the Scripture has said, out of his heart will flow rivers of living water' " (John 7:38), and then he explains, "This He spoke concerning the Spirit" (verse 39).

The farmers of Israel began plowing their fields and sowing their seed in the middle of October, shortly after the falling of the early rains. These rains enabled the seed to germinate, and they nurtured its early growth. The latter rain came in the late spring. It brought the grain to full growth.

The early rain of the Spirit fell upon the disciples at Pentecost, launching the Christian church, and the corresponding latter rain will be poured out on God's church at the end time to bring His work on earth to full fruition. When it falls, the church will receive the power to complete God's mission on earth. Through the outpouring of the Holy Spirit in latter-rain power, the earth will be illuminated with the glory of God.

That outpouring will be the greatest manifestation of the Holy Spirit's power since Pentecost. The light of God's Word will penetrate the darkest corners of this earth. His love will be revealed in His people, showing to a waiting world and a watching universe that His grace is sufficient to enable even sinners to overcome all the powers of evil. As God's power works in the lives of His people, His message will triumph and Jesus will come (Matthew 24:14).

It will take nothing less than latter-rain power for the church to complete God's mission on earth, and God offers nothing less than that power. God gives us an infinite supply of Heaven's most precious gift to enable His church to accomplish the most urgent and important task ever entrusted to human beings.

The great controversy ended

Revelation, the Bible's last book, records God's final message to a planet in deep trouble. God's last appeal is full of hope. The message of the entire book of Revelation can be summarized in just four words: Jesus wins; Satan loses. All of history is moving to a glorious climax—the coming of Jesus. He will return to earth as King of kings and Lord of lords.

This is good news. In fact, it is the most incredible news in the whole universe. The same Jesus who went to the cross to defeat Satan will come again and triumph over the powers of hell to make a full end of evil. (See Revelation 19:19–21; Ezekiel 28:18, 19.) Evil won't have the last word. Poverty and pestilence won't have the last word. Sickness and suffering won't have the last word. Chaos and crime won't have the last word. Disease and death won't have the last word. God will have the last word. He will write the final chapter of the controversy between good and evil.

Why hasn't He already done so? Because God wants to save as many people as possible. He loves lost people. Because His love is infinite, He cannot bear the thought of one person being lost. So, the Father, Son, and Holy Spirit are unitedly doing everything possible to reach every person.

Soon the final crisis will break upon this world. Soon Jesus will pour out His Spirit in latter-rain power and the work of God on earth will be finished. Soon "servants of God, with their faces lighted up and shining with holy consecration, will hasten from place to place to proclaim the message from heaven. By thousands of voices, all over the earth, the warning will be given. Miracles will be wrought, the sick will be healed, and signs and wonders will follow the believers."[6]

Soon Jesus will come. Soon all heaven and earth will rejoice. Since all this will happen so soon, there is nothing more important than our experiencing a revival of God's grace in our hearts daily and our inviting His Holy Spirit to reform us into His image (1 John 3:1–3).

Will you open your heart to Jesus right now and ask Him to do a deep work of grace in your life? Will you renew your commitment to pray, study the Bible, and witness? Will you surrender everything in your life that the Holy Spirit points out is not in harmony with God's will? Join me in making this commitment right now.

1. Ellen G. White, *The Desire of Ages,* 611.
2. White, *Christ's Object Lessons,* 121.
3. White, *The Acts of the Apostles,* 50; emphasis added.
4. White, *Review and Herald,* August 25, 1896.
5. White, *Testimonies for the Church,* 8:23.
6. White, *The Great Controversy,* 612.

Revive Us Again
by Mark A. Finley

There is nothing that the Seventh-day Adventist Church needs more than a genuine spiritual revival. There is nothing that Satan fears more than this promised revival.

In *Revive Us Again*, Pastor Mark Finley invites you to prayerfully open your heart and mind. Revival always begins with one man, one woman, one boy, or one girl on his or her knees, seeking God. You can be that one person who is used of God to bring the outpouring of the Holy Spirit on your home, your church, and your world.

Hardcover, 128 Pages
ISBN 13: 978-0-8163-2450-7
ISBN 10: 0-8163-2450-6

10 Days in the Upper Room
Mark A. Finley

Have you ever wondered why the disciples had such death-defying faith? What was it that gave them the courage to proclaim the gospel to the ends of the earth in spite of the overwhelming challenges? All of Heaven is waiting for God's people to be ready to receive this power so He can finish His work on earth and take His children home. *10 Days in the Upper Room* can lead you into a life-transforming experience.

96 Pages
ISBN 13: 978-0-8163-2487-3
ISBN 10: 0-8163-2487-5

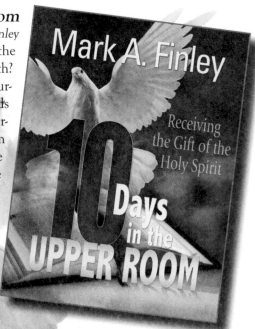

Pacific Press®
Publishing Association
"Where the Word Is Life"

Three ways to order:

1	Local	Adventist Book Center®
2	Call	1-800-765-6955
3	Shop	AdventistBookCenter.com